WALKING THE LINE

NICOLA MARSH

Copyright © Nicola Marsh 2015
Published by Nicola Marsh 2015

All the characters in this book have no existence outside the imagination of the author and have no relation whatsoever to anyone bearing the same name or names. They're not distantly inspired by any individual known or unknown to the author and all the incidents in the book are pure invention.

All rights reserved including the right of reproduction in any form. The text or any part of the publication may not be reproduced or transmitted in any form without the written permission of the publisher.

The author acknowledges the copyrighted or trademarked status and trademark owners of the word marks mentioned in this work of fiction.

With a name like Finn Ahearn, my Irish luck should be guaranteed. Instead, it runs out when I travel half way around the world to Sydney. The seedier side of King's Cross catches up with me and the only way I can get back on stable footing is to accept a job as a bartender, working for the tough Aussie owner Ellie Finch.

Ellie's a decade older than me and tries to resist my charms. She doesn't believe in happily ever-after because hers imploded a long time ago, our values are worlds apart, and we have nothing in common.

But I'm a smooth-talking Irishman and I'm determined to sway a hard-hearted cynic to believe in love again.

ONE

FINN

The fabled Irish luck my homeland is famous for? A leprechaun's crock of shit.

Since I'd landed in Sydney yesterday I'd had my pockets picked, lost my passport, had my secret stash of cash stolen and was about to get my head kicked in by a bunch of lowlifes hanging around the fountain at Kings Cross.

Four ferals wearing hoodies that hadn't seen the inside of a washing machine for a month stalked toward me, hands in pockets, trouble in their frigid glares.

I hesitated, glanced at the park behind me, knowing that making a run for it wouldn't stop this rabble. They looked meaner than my Aunt Siobhan when her whiskey soured.

I had no choice. I had to cut through the group to get to the backpackers' hostel at the other end of Darlinghurst Road. And that meant I was definitely cruising for a bruising.

As I squared my shoulders and tried to make the most of my six feet two inches—yeah, like height trumped weapons—I wished for a fleeting second I was back in Cork, sitting down to one of Mum's famous stews alongside my six siblings, a raggedy mob who bickered over anything from Gaelic football results to the state of the economy.

My family drove me nuts, but the last thing they needed was to get a long distance phone call reporting I'd been beaten up. Or worse.

Cursing my idiocy at wanting to experience more beyond the charmed life I'd led in Cork, I strode toward the gang.

"Hey mate, you're late." A young guy stepped out of a doorway on my left and clapped me on the back. "The rest of the guys are inside waiting for us."

I had no idea who this guy was but as the ferals frowned and their narrow-eyed gazes flicked between us in confusion, I knew I'd rather take my chances heading into the bar with my new bestie.

I made a grand show of glancing at my watch. "Sorry. Didn't think rugby training would finish so late."

The young guy grinned, appearing suitably impressed by my quick improvisation. "Come on. Next round's on you."

I gladly followed the guy into the bar, hoping he didn't have ten biker mates in the back room who'd do worse than the gang outside.

After scouring countless websites citing Kings Cross as raw and edgy and real, I'd known this is where I would kick off my Aussie trip. Way past time for this good Catholic boy to get down and dirty and what better place than the Cross, as locals called it. I'd expected the strip club spruikers, druggies, drunks, pimps, prostitutes, transvestites and dealers. I hadn't expected to feel so goddamn vulnerable.

"First day in Oz?" the guy asked, as we stepped into a surprisingly empty bar, considering dusk brought the crowds out along this strip.

"Second," I said, managing a wry smile. "What gave it away?"

"The fact you were dumb enough to take on four guys unarmed instead of taking refuge in a bar 'til they left." The guy stuck his hand out. "Kye Sheldon."

"Finn Ahearn, clueless Irish mick who thanks you for saving my arse."

Kye grinned. "You're welcome." He slid behind the bar. "Beer?"

I nodded. "You work here?"

"Nah, but I've known Ellie for years, she won't mind." He pulled two beers like a barman, leaving the right amount of head. "She loves it when I visit."

"Ellie's the owner?"

"Yeah, she's the best." Kye slid a beer toward me. "We used to be neighbors."

A local had rescued me. Made sense the gang had backed off rather than attacking us. They probably sensed a kindred spirit, though Kye looked far from a hoodlum. In fact, he could've been a double for one of the Hemsworth dudes my youngest sis was always drooling over.

"You lived here?" Unfortunately, I made it sound like he'd grown up in the gutter and a frown slashed his brows.

"My Mum ran the strip joint next door. We lived in the apartment above." Kye's flat tone held so much coldness I almost shivered. "She died five years ago, when I was fifteen."

I wanted to say sorry but knew this kid wouldn't want a trite apology.

"Sounds tough, losing her so young."

"I survived." Kye drained his beer in a few short gulps. "Which is more than I can say for you if you keep wandering around the Cross with 'tourist' tattooed on your forehead."

He narrowed his eyes, glared at me. "No offence, mate, but you look like a kid waiting to be beat up."

Bane of my existence, looking like a teenager. Mum's genes. Dad resembled a Sharpay.

"I'm twenty-four."

Kye's eyebrows rose. "No shit?"

I chuckled, liking Kye's forthrightness. "I get enough of that from my six siblings."

"Six, fuck." Kye winced. "Let me guess. Good Catholic family?"

I nodded. "Born and bred in Cork, five generations."

"What brings you here?"

I'd been pondering that very question for months. The simple answer was the four-month turf management job I'd been offered courtesy of my granddad's connections. I didn't want to think about the rest right now, so I settled for simple.

"Job offer in Melbourne to up-skill, couldn't say no."

Kye tilted his head slightly, studying me, like he sensed I was full of BS. "What do you do?"

"Specialty turf management for sporting grounds. You?"

"Tennis player."

From where I came from, tennis was a hobby, and my skepticism must've showed because Kye sniggered.

"I know, right? Imagine getting paid to play sport."

"You must be good."

He shrugged. "Been at the academy two years. It's a shithole."

"Then why do you stick at it?"

Damn, the question popped out before I could stop. My bluntness was something I'd tried to conquer my whole life and failed, despite several black eyes and the odd case of blue balls spurring me on.

"Because I can't do anything else." Rather than punch me in the head, Kye eyed me with newfound respect. "How long are you in Sydney for?"

"A month. Thought I'd do the touristy thing 'til the job starts. Though considering I had the bulk of my savings stolen by some hippy chick I was drinking with last night, I may have to cut my time in Sydney short."

Kye hesitated, as if weighing his words carefully. "Where are you staying?"

My thumb jerked at the door. "One of the backpacker hostels on Darlinghurst Road."

"You won't last a week."

Annoyed by his accurate assumption, considering what had occurred over the last twenty-four hours, I rested my forearms on the bar.

"Guess that's my problem, not yours."

Kye frowned and glanced over his shoulder at a huge mirrored glass window at the back of the bar. "Actually, I think I have a solution to your problem."

"What—"

"Ever worked in a bar?"

I rolled my eyes. "I'm Irish. What do you think?"

"I take that as a yes?"

I nodded, increasingly confused.

"You need to lose the deer-in-the-headlights expression

for locals to respect you. Plus you need money." Kye pulled me another beer though I'd barely touched the first. "Here, get this into you while I have a chat to Ellie."

He grinned. "If Ellie can't toughen you up, no-one can."

~

ELLIE

AS KYE STUCK his head around my office door, I pointed at the bar where he'd left his mate. "Hope you left your money in the till."

Kye grinned. "What happened to your beers on the house policy?"

"That only applies to you, not some stray you drag in here when we're officially closed." I stood and moved around the desk, beckoning him in. "Who is he?"

"Irishman who was about to get his head kicked in."

"So you saved him?" I clutched at my chest. "Careful there, Squirt, you're almost making me believe you have a heart."

"You've known me long enough to know that's bullshit." Kye entered the office and made a beeline for me. "How've you been?"

"Can't complain."

He hugged me and I swallowed the lump that inevitably lodged in my throat whenever Kye visited.

I'd known him for fifteen years, since I'd lobbed in the Cross and started working here. He'd been a cherubic five year old who'd made my heart bleed for what I'd left behind and what I could never have. Sheree, his mum, had been instrumental in me eventually buying the bar so after she'd died, I'd made a personal vow to look after Kye best I could.

He'd left the Cross five years ago, sent off to boarding school by his rich dad, then lived at the fancy-schmancy tennis academy the last two years. But Kye never forgot his roots and often came to visit, usually dropping by unexpectedly, like now. Highlight of my shitty week so far. Casual employees and their fickleness sucked; trying to make the roster work when down two workers was a major pain in the arse.

He released me, and held me at arm's length. "You look tired."

"Pulling extra shifts to fill in for flaky shitheads will do that to a girl." I gestured at my desk. "Plus I'm way behind on paperwork because of it."

A slow grin creased his face. "I might have the answer to your problems."

"Unless you have Ryan Gosling willing to pull beers for an evening before tucking me into bed, I'm not interested."

Kye laughed. "The Irishman knows how to work a bar and he needs a cash injection."

"No." I held up my hand. "I don't hire tourists."

"He has a working visa. Heading down to Melbourne in a month." Kye pointed at the glass. "He can help you out of your staff shortage fix and you can provide him with something he needs more than money."

"What's that?"

"Life experience." Kye's audible concern surprised me. "The guy's a patsy. An easy mark." His eyes narrowed, suddenly sly. "You know what that's like, right?"

"Touché." I'd almost been mugged—and worse—by one of Sheree's drunk patrons when I'd first arrived at the Cross, a naive country girl who'd run from my past, seeking refuge in the big city. Small town life hadn't prepared me for Sydney but I'd wised up, learned, adapted, thanks to Sheree and my job here.

Maybe I should do the same for the Irishman? Pay it forward and all that karma crap.

"Working here will give the guy some experience of the Cross, so he's not picked off before the week's out." Kye snickered. "Plus I feel sorry for him."

"He's that clueless?"

"Worse. One of those annoyingly cheerful optimists, the exact opposite of us."

"Ugh. Don't you hate that?"

Kye grinned. "Shit yeah. The guy needs a mentor—"

"And that's you?" I snorted. "You'll have him corrupted in less than a day."

Kye chuckled. "Reckon he needs me to be his new bestie and that means I'll be visiting you all the time."

"Blackmail, Squirt, seriously?" I laughed at his faux angelic expression. "Come on, what's your angle on this? Tell me the truth and I might consider hiring him."

Kye's amused expression faded. "We're two of a kind, El. Jaded cynics that can spot a shyster at twenty paces." He jerked his head at the glass. "We don't trust lightly but I could tell in the first five minutes that Finn's one of the good guys."

I snorted. "Finn? Could he be any more clichéd?"

"He is Irish." Puzzled, Kye searched my face, as if he couldn't quite gauge my mood. "With the accent to prove it."

I wasn't convinced that hiring an ingenuous Irishman was the answer to my staffing problems but it would get me out of a bind until I could hire someone more permanent.

And Kye was right. I didn't trust many people but I did trust his judgment. Guess I had myself a new employee.

I found myself reluctantly nodding. "Okay. Introduce me to this guy who's going to save my arse."

Kye winked. "And what a fine arse it is, I might add."

I punched him in the arm, hard, and we elbowed each other as we headed into the bar.

TWO

ELLIE

My first thought on seeing Finn as he swiveled on the bar stool to face me was *emerald eyes, seriously, aren't you taking the Irish cliché to extremes?*

Though technically his eyes weren't green, more a combination of blue and jade, resulting in a startling aquamarine that left me a little breathless. And I never lost my breath over a guy. Not anymore.

Kye gestured between us. "Finn Ahearn, meet Ellie Finch."

Then Finn had to go and smile and dammit, he had a dimple.

"Nice to meet you, Ellie." He stuck out his hand and I stared at it, shaken to my core.

That voice. That accent. Like Sean Connery and Alan Rickman slugging it out in an audition to star in an Irish feature film. So damn sexy.

I didn't want to admit it, but I tingled. Down there. In a way I hadn't tingled in a *looooong* time.

"You too." I shook his hand, releasing it as fast as humanly possible, earning a raised eyebrow and sardonic twist of his lips.

His lips...full. Sensual. Kissable.

What the hell was wrong with me?

I didn't lust over guys. I had the occasional meaningless one night stand to scratch a physical itch. Guys who knew the score. Bonking buddies. Guys far removed from Finn, an intriguing blend of innocence and charm, like he wanted to be naughty but didn't know how to do it.

Time to cut my losses and run.

"Ellie's short-staffed and I thought you might want to help her out." Kye slapped Finn on the back and damned if the both of them didn't look at me like some life-saving angel.

So much for reneging.

"Can you start tonight?" Once again, I sounded harsh and mean, but rather than get defensive as most people did around me, Finn actually laughed.

"Absolutely." He leaned forward a little, amusement quirking his mouth. "If you personally show me the ropes, that is."

Oh my God. The guy was flirting with me? In front of Kye? I'd never hear the end of it.

"Come back at seven. We open at eight." I looked him up and down, wishing I hadn't. Lean legs, zero abdominal body fat, decent pecs and biceps a girl could grip onto while riding him all night long.

That observation was so not helping.

I probably needed to get laid. It had been about four months. Not that I counted or cared. But if my reaction to the Irishman I'd just met was any indication, I needed to do the horizontal shimmy with a buddy sooner rather than later.

"Wear black pants and a white shirt," I said, turning on my heel and stalking back toward the office. Not before I'd seen Kye's knowing smirk.

Damn, the kid knew me too well. I was rattled and it showed.

"Thanks, Ellie," Kye called out, a teasing lilt in his voice, and I raised my hand without looking back.

"See you later," Finn said, and damned if my insides didn't quiver. The deep, sexy voice was bad enough. Throw in the charming accent and all I wanted to do was turn around and fire him before he'd started.

I made it to the safety of my office and slammed the door. It didn't help the uncertainty churning my gut as I looked out through the one-way mirrored window, wondering what the hell I'd just done.

THREE

FINN

Things were looking up. My passport had been located near a bin at Circular Quay and the local police had called. I had a job to replenish my meager cash stocks. And with any luck, if I played my cards right, according to Kye I could have a better living situation by the end of tonight.

But first, I had to charm Ellie.

Considering she seemed to hate me on sight, it could be tough. But I relished a challenge and when Kye had mentioned she had a spare room above the bar that she occasionally rented out, I knew what had to be done.

Impress with my work ethic, rake in a stash of tips and appeal to her gentle side. If she had one. I'd never met a more prickly person. But the fact she'd given me a chance at a job when Kye had asked meant there had to be a softer side beneath the short spiky blonde hair, kohl-rimmed blue eyes, vivid red-slicked lips and black leather.

She would've intimidated me once, that kind of brash, bold woman. But I was through being the perfect son who dated the perfect woman. I couldn't be that guy anymore. Not for my family. Not for me. And there was something about Ellie that intrigued me on an intrinsic level. I'd felt sucker-punched in the gut when she'd first looked at me, all wary defiance, as if she expected me to punch back and would come out swinging.

So I'd done what came naturally. Flirted. Kye had later mentioned I was lucky Ellie hadn't kneed me in the balls on the spot. But Kye had also mentioned he'd never seen Ellie so defensive, which meant I'd crept under her guard. Something I intended on doing throughout my training, starting now, as I caught sight of her coming down the stairs tucked into the back corner.

The first thing I noticed, she'd changed. Swapped the black leather pants and jacket for a red, skin-tight leather mini and a crimson bustier that pushed her tits up to create an eye-popping cleavage. The second thing? She hadn't lost the scowl but my rock-hard cock didn't seem to care.

"What are you staring at?" She marched behind the bar, rested her hands on it, and glared.

"You look incredible," I said, the simple truth not garnering any change in expression from her. So I switched to charm. "Can't a guy appreciate the beauty of a woman?" I didn't add, 'without getting his head snapped off.'

"You're full of shit," she said, sounding utterly disgusted. "Now do you want to learn the ropes or not?"

"I'm all yours." I stepped around the bar to stand close. Close enough to smell an alluring fragrance reminiscent of the short stopover I'd had in Hong Kong: Oriental, mysterious, heady. "Do your worst."

She stiffened, her squared shoulders giving me another

eyeful of that enticing cleavage. "Cut the bullshit flirting, okay? I'm immune." She tapped her watch. "Save it for the customers, who'll be arriving in less than an hour."

Rather than give in, I pushed myself up onto the bar, sitting on it so I could face her. "Don't you like flirting?"

"What do you think, Einstein?" Her withering stare would've shriveled the balls on a lesser man. But I wasn't backing down. I needed to be in that room over the bar later tonight and that meant whittling away at her defenses, one quip at a time.

She puffed out a long breath. "Look, it's been a long week. You either want this job or not. Me? I don't give a shit but Kye's a good guy and he asked me to hire you as a favor." She pointed at the beer kegs. "So you either get your arse off my bar and start showing me what you've got or you can piss off."

I'd like to show her what I had but then I'd be back to square one: no money and living in that hellhole hostel.

Appearing suitably chastised, I slid off the bar and landed on my feet. "I appreciate the job. And Kye is a good guy, because for some unknown reason he took pity on an idiot Irishman this afternoon, not only preventing me getting bashed, but getting me this job too. So thanks."

Her response was a brief nod but I noted the softening around her mouth.

"I've worked in pubs back home, so I'm used to pulling a pint or two."

At last, she looked at me, and she'd lost the mean glitter in her eyes. "Where you from?"

"Cork. Ever been to Ireland?"

For a second I swore I glimpsed sadness lurking in those big, blue eyes before she shook her head.

"So you've lived in Sydney your whole life?"

She hesitated, glanced away. "Came here in my late teens. Was a small town girl before that. Never travelled."

"Me either. This is my first trip and I only came here because..." I trailed off, not wanting to divulge the entire truth, because it'd make me sound like a sissy.

"Because?" she prompted, staring at me with interest. At least I had her full attention.

"Because my family wants to migrate here and my grandfather pulled strings to get me a turf management position as a way of testing the lay of the land."

To my astonishment, the corners of her mouth curved into a semi-smile. "You're their scout? Checking that we don't have kangaroos roaming the city streets?"

"Yeah, go figure." I smiled and for a long, drawn out moment it felt like we connected. "Lucky for you, I'm no boy scout."

Rather than bristle and shut down as expected, she rolled her eyes. "That pesky flirting is just part of your Irish charm, isn't it?"

I leaned in closer, buoyed when she didn't edge away. "Is it working?"

"Hell no," she said a tad loudly and I laughed.

"Guess I'll have to keep trying then."

She held up both hands. "Please don't."

"Nice to know you think I'm charming though." I winked. "Gives a guy something to work on."

"The only work you'll be doing around here is this." She gestured at the bar. "I'll show you where everything is, watch you pull a few beers, then throw you in the deep end."

"I'm up for it."

For the second time in as many minutes our gazes locked. Hot. Loaded. Potent.

And suddenly, gaining access to the room upstairs was more than having a decent place to stay.

It meant I'd be closer to Ellie.

FOUR

ELLIE

Working with Finn was hell.

Pure, yanking-out-eyebrow-hairs-one-at-a-time, Brazilian-wax, torturous hell.

Being understaffed, I'd had to work the bar alongside him tonight. So I'd been privy to his constant sexy smiles, his incessant flirting and the panty-dropping charm that seemed to come as natural to him as breathing.

And while he did it with everyone, he seemed to focus most of it on me. I'd tried freezing him out, shooting death glares, even the odd name-calling. The result? He tried harder. What was worse, I actually liked it.

I didn't flirt. I didn't encourage guys. I donned my armor every morning, from my foundation to the five ring piercings in each ear, and faced the world head on. That was another thing; when I'd walked downstairs earlier, the way he'd looked at me seemed like he could see beneath my deliberately chosen leather exterior to the real me beneath. It had disarmed me more than anything and I'd wanted to fire him on the spot.

Kye had been right about the optimism thing too. I'd heard Finn say he'd had his money stolen by some chick at the backpackers' where he was staying, had lost his passport and had his pockets picked, but then he'd waxed lyrical about Sydney and made the crappy stuff sound insignificant.

The guy was one of those annoyingly chipper people who bounced through life with a permanent smile on their face, oblivious to the darker realities. I couldn't stand that kind of blatant cheeriness. It grated. And made me want to shake some sense into him.

But then Finn would turn some of that warm liveliness on me and for an all-too-brief second I'd forget the reasons why I'd morphed into a hard bitch and allow myself the luxury of basking in his all's-right-with-the-world happiness.

Eager to get the hell away from him, I slid the last bolt home on the front door. "I'll pay you for tonight then you can leave out the back."

"Actually, could we talk?"

Liquid warmth pooled in places it shouldn't and I inwardly cursed my body's reaction to his voice. "What's up?"

"Firstly, aren't you going to commend me on a stellar job?" He grinned like a proud little boy who'd mastered toilet training. "Several of those customers said they were moving on to other clubs but ended up staying here all night."

Annoyed that he was right, I crossed my arms. "And you think that's because of you?"

"Damn right." He perched on a bar stool and patted the one next to him. "They enjoy my flirtatious charm as much as you do."

I frowned. "But I don't."

"Liar," he said, so softly my skin rippled with goosebumps. "You love my charm."

I snorted and reluctantly took a seat beside him, only because my new three-inch heels had murdered my feet. "You can turn it off now. Your audience has left."

"Why don't I turn it on instead?"

Before I could blink he'd placed his hands either side of my barstool, effectively pinning me between the bar and his all-too-close body.

Bamboozled by his nearness, the lust in his eyes and the intoxicating scent of hard-working male sweat and woodsy aftershave, I blurted the first thing that popped into my head.

"I'm thirty-four."

"You look twenty-four." He smiled and I resisted the urge to dip my finger into that captivating dimple. "My age, in case you needed more ammunition to keep me at arm's length."

He was a decade younger than me? Jeez. Not that I had any intention of robbing a cradle, even a cute Irish one, but the fact we were ten years apart merely accentuated the divide between us.

I dragged in a deep breath, immediately wishing I hadn't when my lungs filled with him. "Move."

He leaned in closer. "Only if you ask nicely."

"Don't make me hurt you."

It sounded childish, an empty threat that made him laugh.

"Like to see you try, babe."

"I just bet you would." I glanced away, irritated by the heat flooding my body and rising into my cheeks. "It's been a long day, so could you please just shut up and—"

"I'm staying."

"Excuse me?"

There was ballsy and charming, and then there was certifiably insane. No way would I have a one-night stand with a guy I'd only just met; who happened to be my employee.

"Kye said you had a room upstairs you occasionally rent?" To my relief, he leaned back, releasing me from my not-totally-unwelcome prison. "I'm low on funds and have a feeling any cash I earn from here will disappear as fast in that hostel where I'm staying, so..." He tried one of his signature smiles and damn if it didn't melt me a little. "I was hoping you'd help me out."

If working alongside Finn had been hell, having him across the hall from me upstairs would be madness. But the longer he stared at me with those guileless eyes filled with hope, the harder it was to say no.

Steeling my resolve against Irish charmers, I shook my head. "No."

His mouth quirked into a wry grin. "Need some time to think about that?"

I paused and tapped my temple pretending to think. "Uh...the answer's still no."

"It could be fun..." He leaned forward again and this time I laid a hand on his chest and shoved him backwards. "Or not." He laughed, the deep reverberations reaching down to my soul. Where no man would ever touch again.

"Come into the office, I'll pay you, and you can go." I tried to stand, desperate to escape our nearness, but his knees bumped mine and I ended up almost on the floor.

"Okay, but not before this."

His arms shot out to steady me, then he hauled me closer. Close enough I could see his stubble was a shade lighter than his auburn-blonde hair. Close enough I could see indigo flecks in his green eyes. Close enough I could see a tiny scar on the outer corner of his right eyebrow.

"Let me go—"

He kissed me. Snatching my breath. Stealing my sanity. Sealing my fate.

Because as Finn's lips moved against mine and his tongue demanded entrance I was foolishly willing to give, I could think of nothing but the heat, the pleasure, the desire to experience this and so much more.

Our teeth clashed a little. Our noses bumped. It didn't matter. What Finn lacked in finesse he more than made up for with enthusiasm. I'd never been ravaged like this before, as if he couldn't get enough. It was pretty damn intoxicating for a hardened cynic.

I started to pull away but he wouldn't let me, deepening the kiss until I was consumed. Unable to think of anything else but being in this moment, somewhat grateful to turn off the cold, hard, logical part of me and turn on the womanly desires I'd long suppressed.

"Let me stay," he murmured against my mouth, a second before his hand palmed my breast.

I groaned at the same time reality set in, his plea serving as a douse of icy water.

Of course that's what the kiss had been about. A way of sweetening me up.

God, I was such a fool, believing for a moment that this sweet, young guy could want me. I should know better by now but looked like my past mistakes had taught me nothing.

I shoved and he released me, managing to look guilty and angelic simultaneously. "Get out."

"Not 'til you agree to let me stay."

I shook my head, annoyed by the uncharacteristic burn of tears behind my eyes. "You're a piece of work, thinking one lousy kiss would sway me to change my mind."

Confusion clouded his expression, before I glimpsed hurt. "That's not why I kissed you."

"Then why did you?"

"Because I've wanted to do it all frigging day, sweetheart, from the moment you strutted out here this morning." He grabbed my hand and pressed it against his fly. Yowza. Impressive bulge. "I want you. And I'm sick of spending my life not saying what I really want because of what other people may think."

All too soon, he released my hand and I surreptitiously flexed my fingers at the loss of heat. "You won't understand but being the perfect son, the eternal nice guy, gets you frigging nowhere."

Damn, he'd done it again, honing in on my weak spot without knowing. Because I did understand how being a good person got you nowhere. It's exactly what had happened to me, why I'd left Dubbo to start afresh in Sydney.

My Mr. Nice had crapped on me from a great height, leaving my dreams shattered and my life in tatters. Being naive, trusting and nice sucked, which is why I'd done everything in my power to be the exact opposite in my new life here. So why the hell was I contemplating taking a softer approach on this guy, just because I felt an unwelcome empathy?

"Look, Ellie, you've been great to me today, throwing me a lifeline with this job 'til I replenish my bank balance."

He rubbed a hand over his face, before eyeballing me with his too-honest stare. "You're hot. That's why I kissed you. End of story."

He pointed upstairs. "As for the room, consider it your good deed for the day, taking pity on a dumb schmuck who trusts too easily."

Hated to admit it, but his bluntness got to me as much as his charm. And a small part of me really wanted to believe he kissed me because of the underlying spark between us. I shouldn't believe him, I wouldn't, but what if for the short time he was in Sydney I could...

"Already done my good deed for the day, giving you a job in the first place," I said, my gruffness hiding how much I liked his refreshing honesty.

He smiled and damned if I didn't want to kiss him again. "Haven't you heard? Do an Irishman a favor, you'll have luck for a week. Do him another, and you'll get really lucky."

I didn't need to see the naughty gleam in his eyes to know how he wanted to get lucky with me.

"You're a pain in the arse," I said, shaking my head, on the verge of admitting defeat. It must've shown, because he grinned like I'd handed him the keys to the Opera House.

"And you're the best." He swooped in and kissed me on the cheek, before doing an Irish jig that had me laughing against my better judgment. "I'll crash here tonight and get my stuff in the morning."

"Technically, I haven't said yes."

"But you want to." He cupped my cheek, his thumb brushing my lower lip and I couldn't have moved if I wanted to. "I like you, Ellie Finch."

As he lowered his head to brush his lips across mine, a little voice inside my head whispered, 'I like you too'.

This time, his kiss was soft and tender, over before it had begun, leaving me wanting more.

"Go out with me," he said, snagging my hand. "A date. Somewhere nice."

"Thought you were broke?"

The corners of his mouth curved upward. "Romance doesn't require a lot of dollars."

"Romance?" I snorted. "Maybe you were right about being a dumb schmuck."

"Don't you believe in it?"

I blew a raspberry.

"I'll take that as a no." He chuckled and squeezed my hand, surprising me when I realized I hadn't yanked away from him yet.

"I don't date."

His eyebrows shot up. "Ever?"

"Not interested."

"In guys?" he asked, a teasing lilt in his voice.

"In mess." This time I succeeded in pulling my hand out of his.

"It's just a date." He reached for me again and I sidestepped.

"And my answer's still no."

I headed for the back to lock up before he could undermine me further with those mischievous eyes and delectable dimple.

"You know I'll keep asking, right?" he called out.

"Not going to change my mind," I said, ignoring the way his taunting chuckles made my insides clench with desire and made me want to yell 'hell yeah' to any damn question he may ask.

FIVE

FINN

I wiped down the bar, watching Kye hustle a drunk preppy businessman out the door.

It had been his third eviction of the night and Ellie didn't seem to mind. In fact, she had that adoring look most women had for heroic deeds. Yeah, like being an unofficial bouncer was so hard.

Kye waited by the front door as the last two patrons, barely legal women who'd ingested too many Margaritas, tottered out into the cesspool that was Kings Cross at night.

In the week I'd been here, I'd seen crowds stream along Darlinghurst Road, particularly between eleven pm and two am, when Ellie closed on the weekends. She'd casually mentioned the Cross had the highest murder and crime stats in the city and with some of the lowlifes I'd seen, I could believe it. What intrigued me though were the hip inner city types strolling alongside them, searching for entertainment, good food or a drink.

The Cross was intriguingly cosmopolitan and now that I was working here I loved its vibe, perfect for a guy like me to discover there was more to life than Mum's weekly Sunday roast and potato stew.

What I didn't love was Ellie's tough outer shell. I hadn't been able to wear her down into accepting a date. In fact, over the last seven days, she'd done her best to avoid me. When I worked, she didn't. When I was upstairs, she was out or hiding away in her apartment, which I gleaned was an unexpected bonus of staying here; she lived upstairs too. When I spoke to her, she kept her responses terse.

Gone was the woman who'd kissed me like she couldn't get enough, the softer woman who'd given an idiot a break.

Which meant one thing. I needed to enlist the help of her golden boy.

"You're in a bad mood," I said, as Kye finished locking up and took a seat at the bar. "That time of the month?"

"Fuck off." He pinched the bridge of his nose. "God, I hate those yuppie pricks."

Sensing there was more behind Kye's intense dislike of guys in suits, I casually asked, "Why?"

"Because they're all the same." He scowled. "They're like the privileged pricks I went to boarding school with. The type of rich arseholes who said horrible things about my Mum because of what she did, about the girls who worked at her club."

Kye's fingers clenched into fists. "Those idiots didn't have a clue that most of the women who stripped were funding their way through uni or single mums trying to make ends meet."

He jabbed a finger toward the door. "The dickheads who come in here, getting liquored up before they head down the street to a live sex show are those narrow-minded, judgmental students grown up." He shook his head. "Makes me so fucking mad."

"Easy there, big fella." I pulled a beer and slid it across to him. "Sounds like you need this."

Kye nodded his thanks, but he hadn't lost the tightness around his mouth or the clenched jaw. "I get this way sometimes."

"Mad at the injustices of the world?"

"Just mad. Crazy angry..." he trailed off, his fingers wrapped around the glass so tight I wondered if it'd break. "It's why I picked up a tennis racket in the first place, to work off my frustration."

"How old were you?"

"Thirteen.

I whistled low. "You've been an angry son-of-a-bitch for seven years?"

"Helps on the court," he said, with a casual shrug. "Plus no dweeb wants to approach me at the academy."

I stared at Kye with a newfound respect. He may be four years younger than me but attitude-wise he was years ahead. "Tell me this. If you're so angry all the time, why didn't you slug me that first day?"

"Because you're a pussy." For the first time all night, Kye grinned. "Who knows, maybe you're so soft you brought out the sensitive new age guy in me?"

I laughed. "Care to put your inner SNAG to good use?"

"Don't push your luck," he said, draining half his beer in two gulps.

"I need help with Ellie."

Kye put his beer down, suddenly serious. "Is she okay?"

I nodded. "She won't say yes to a date with me."

Kye's mouth stretched into an ear-splitting grin. "That's why she's been hiding away this week?"

"You noticed?"

"Hell yeah. Barely seen her. She's constantly busy with replenishing stock or meeting with new distributors or some crap."

"You're not mad?" I started stacking beer glasses upside down on a tray. "You two are close and I thought you might have a problem with me dating her."

Kye shook his head. "Mate, she's been a second mum to me and I'd deliver her hogtied at your feet if I could."

Relieved that Kye had just confirmed there was nothing more than friendship between him and Ellie, I chuckled. "Is that your way of saying she needs a date real bad?"

Kye paused, staring into his beer, as if contemplating the wisdom of saying more. I waited, trusting the guy who knew Ellie well to give me some sound advice.

When Kye eyeballed me, I knew whatever he had to say would give me some much needed insight into the woman who invaded my dreams and kept me up most nights.

"Ellie's like me. A tough cynic who expects the worst from people and can't handle the good." Kye swiped at the condensation on his glass. "People like you, with stars in your eyes, make us uncomfortable. You're so upbeat all the time, so damn trusting, but the world doesn't work that way, and Ellie and me know it."

A light bulb went off and I knew what he'd say next.

"That's why I saved your arse that first day. And why I got you the job here."

"Because you think I'm a naive fool?"

"Because you're one of the good guys who needs a bit of life experience to get you through your stay in Sydney without getting your head kicked in." Kye drained the rest of his beer and handed me the glass. "Ellie needs a good guy in her life, even for a short time, and that's why I'm going to help you. I've been angry for less than a decade. For Ellie, it's been longer than that..."

"Go on," I urged, eager to hear more if I was to have any chance of getting through to her.

"She arrived here when I was five. Soon became my mum's best friend so she was around a lot." He gestured around the room. "Started as a barmaid, ended up buying the place after the old owner fell off the perch." He tapped his temple. "Ellie's smart. Resourceful. And way too astute for us. But she wasn't always so closed off..."

I rested my forearms on the bar, waiting, wishing he'd tell me all of it.

"From stuff I overheard when I was older, some guy did a number on her back in Dubbo. Real bad. Bad enough she left her life behind to start fresh here." Kye frowned. "Whoever this dickhead was, he must've hurt her, because she changed and I've watched it happen. Cut her hair short and dyed it. Started wearing leather and chunky jewelry and a ton of make-up. And she never smiled..."

Something in my chest twisted at the thought of anyone hurting Ellie so badly she felt compelled to change who she was.

Kye grimaced. "We don't talk about our pasts much. She probably thinks discussing Mum will make me grumpier than usual and I accept her for who she is now."

He tilted his head, studying me. "That's another thing I respect you for, because I think you do too."

"'Course I do. She's incredible."

"You know she's heaps older than you, right?"

"Yeah, so?"

Kye grinned. "Good answer. So, what can I do to help?"

I'd done a bit of research and hatched a plan. But it all came down to Kye convincing Ellie, because she sure as hell wouldn't listen to me.

"I need you to tell a little white lie…"

SIX

ELLIE

After a long week, I had plans. Plans that included popcorn, chocolate ice cream and a stack of action flicks.

I'd just settled down with a buttery bowl of goodness in my lap and the remote in my hand when a knock sounded at my door.

I could've sworn my heart stopped.

No way. Couldn't be Finn. I'd warned him that no one ever entered my domain up here and so far he'd kept his distance.

Hadn't stopped him asking me out on the rare occasions we'd seen each other the last seven days. I'd done a stellar job of avoiding him but the guy seemed to have a built in radar for knowing where I'd be next.

So we'd done our usual dance. Him charm and flirt. Me freeze and run.

If he'd had the audacity to knock on my apartment door, I'd castrate him.

Because if I liked Finn downstairs in the bar and had a hard time hiding exactly how much, no way in hell I could resist him in my inner sanctuary.

For that's what my apartment was. A sanctuary. A glimpse into the real me. A place filled with frills and feathers, velvets and satins, cushions and candles and frippery, so at odds with my outer persona that I didn't want anyone getting a look at who I really was deep down.

A woman who'd yearned for this life once: the house, the kids, the husband. A woman who believed in dreams of happily-ever-after. A woman who preferred fine teas to alcohol, who enjoyed baking, who'd do anything for her man.

"Open up, El, I know you're in there."

Kye.

I breathed a sigh of relief and tried to ignore the irrational stab of disappointment it wasn't Finn.

"I'm busy, go away," I yelled, knowing it was futile because I'd never been able to say no to him, not since the day he'd presented me with his first mud pie at age six.

"Maybe you'd prefer if I got Finn to help me break down the door?"

At the mention of the F word, I placed the bowl on the coffee table and bolted out of my seat. I opened the door and peeped around it. "You have two seconds before I head back to my date with Vin Diesel."

"Make it five then I'll get out of your way." Kye did that weird upper lip curl thing that passed for a semi-smile and I stood back, beckoning him in.

His far too astute gaze swept the room, lingering on the DVDs stacked beside the TV. "Not sleeping much, huh?"

"I sleep plenty."

At least, I used to, before a green-eyed Irishman with a hot bod and a voice that could tempt a nun to sin kept invading my dreams. So I'd settled for the easier option: dozing on the couch watching old movies.

"You're full of it." Kye didn't sit, which meant he wasn't staying long. "It's none of my business why you've turned into an insomniac so I'll cut to the chase. You still interested in adding more boutique beers to your range?"

"Yeah."

"There's a new joint in town. Upmarket, in Double Bay. Getting rave reviews everywhere for its menu of the liquid variety."

Okay, so he'd piqued my interest. I was constantly striving to make the bar better and more patrons than ever were asking for beers I hadn't heard of.

"Thought you might want to check it out with me?"

I nodded. "Sounds good."

"Tomorrow night, at seven?"

"I'll be there."

Gave me another excuse not to see Finn who was rostered on every evening for the next week.

"Great, see you then." Kye paused at the door. "You really okay?"

"Why wouldn't I be?"

He pointed at the mega popcorn bowl and tub of chocolate ice cream. "Because I remember when you and Mum used to do this, it meant trouble."

My chest ached at the mention of Sheree. I'd loved her like a sister and missed her every day, even now, five years later.

"Men bond over beers and balls, women love junk food and flicks to unwind."

He did the lip quirk thing again. "Balls?"

"Football. Golf. Snooker."

"Right." He grinned, but I still saw concern in his steady gaze. "That's all this is, unwinding?"

"Yeah." I propped against the back of the sofa, wishing he'd leave so I could get past the sudden urge to bawl.

Because the one person in this world I trusted these days was a twenty-year-old, messed up kid with anger management issues and what did that say about me?

That I never let anyone in. That I needed to lighten up. That I needed a life beyond the bar and my bitterness.

"You know, all those times I'd be pretending to play cars on the floor or do puzzles, I actually just enjoyed being around you and Mum," he said, his gaze clouding with memories. "Those were the best times."

"Yeah, they were." I swallowed and blinked back the sting of tears. "Sheree was an incredible person and you're just like her."

Kye's startled gaze shot to mine. "She was so much better than me—"

"Sheree was street smart and astute, with a marshmallow core."

He sneered. "You think I'm soft?"

"I think you care, despite the tough guy facade you present to the world."

Sadness filled me. It had taken me a long time to come to terms with who I was and Kye still had that ahead of him. "Otherwise you wouldn't have taken Finn under your wing."

After an eternity, he reluctantly nodded. "Don't forget I'm not the only one who presents a tough front." His glance away turned crafty. "Maybe you should take Finn under you…"

I laughed at his less-than-subtle innuendo. "Get out."

"Okay." He saluted. "I'll text you the details for tomorrow night."

I nodded, waiting until Kye had left before returning to my place on the couch and wishing he hadn't put that damn image of Finn being under me into my already overactive imagination.

SEVEN

ELLIE

Kye was a no-show.

Not that the twenty minutes I'd waited here had been a hardship. While Double Bay reeked of exclusivity, Maik's had a more welcoming vibe. Sure, it had the requisite black marble and chrome that trendy bars had these days—and so far removed from my mahogany decor it wasn't funny—but there was a warmth here in the strategically placed Japanese screens and secluded tables that I admired despite the minimalist art and white stone fake fireplaces.

And Kye was right about the beers. I'd sampled four and while I may be well on my way to Tipsyville I now knew what to add to my stock.

When the clock behind the stainless steel bar hit seven-thirty and I'd checked my phone for the umpteenth time to see if he'd answered my texts or call, I gave up on Kye.

I had my head down, rummaging in my bag for cab fare, when someone touched my shoulder.

"Don't go."

I froze and glanced up into Finn's handsome face.

"Have dinner with me." He gripped my elbow. "I've heard the chef's special degustation menu is worth the hefty price."

"You're insane." I yanked my arm free, annoyed I wobbled a little. Shouldn't have had all those beers because for one, crazy second I thought there was nothing I'd like more than to have dinner with Finn in this lovely place. "Besides, I'm meeting Kye and he's due any second."

To my chagrin, Finn grinned and tapped my nose. "Haven't you heard this will grow if you tell fibs?"

"How do you know—"

"Because I asked Kye to set this up." He had the grace to look sheepish. "You're either too busy avoiding me or fobbing me off, so I called in the cavalry."

"I'll kill him," I muttered, secretly impressed Kye had gone to such lengths to get me and the Irishman together. Not that it would stop the verbal flaying he had coming his way.

"Please, Ellie, it's just dinner—"

"No." I slipped into my leather jacket and slung my bag over my shoulder, already eyeing the door.

He shrugged. "Too bad. I've already pre-paid for the degustation and you know how strapped for cash I am. Shame you'd let me lose money because you're in mortal fear of being alone with something this good." He patted himself on the chest and I couldn't stop a reluctant smile.

"Have you really paid or is that another lie you and Kye seem so good at?"

"I've paid. But drinks are on you if it appeases your feminist side."

Guilted into it, I nodded. "Fine. But you're lucky I don't fire your arse for coercing me into this by nefarious methods."

He held up his hands in surrender, the picture of faux innocence, and this time laughter burst from my lips.

Finn grinned at me like I'd just handed him a thousand dollar tip. "Our table's this way."

He placed a guiding hand in the small of my back, something that usually annoyed me with guys. Presumptuous. But with Finn, it merely made me feel safe.

It was probably the beer buzz, but when we sat at a cozy table for two at the back of the bar, a screen increasing the intimacy between us, I didn't mind. In fact, it felt nice.

"This isn't so bad, huh?" He rested his forearms on the table. Strong, lean forearms with a light dusting of auburn hair.

How many times had I surreptitiously stared at him, wondering how it would feel to be held in those arms, to be caressed by those hands? Too many and now, with Finn within touching distance, and my resistance lowered by alcohol, I was in immediate danger of doing something I'd regret.

"Depends on your definition of bad," I said, aiming for flippant, but ending up having to clear my throat when I made the mistake of looking into his eyes.

Damn, he felt it too. This thing between us. Invisible. Intangible. But intense all the same.

"Stop looking at me like that," he said, reaching for a glass of water.

"Like what?" I watched him swallow, even admiring the column of his neck.

"Like you think I'm going to gobble you up."

"I'm not—"

"Yeah, you are." He leaned across the table. "And I promise to gobble you up only if you ask nicely."

Heat surged to my cheeks, and several choice places in between. "Must be true what they say about kissing the Blarney Stone."

"I'm not rambling, sweetheart. I'm just stating facts." He relaxed into his chair and pinned me with an intense stare that left me breathless. "I want you. Naked and hot and panting for me."

I gaped at him, stunned by how fiercely I wanted that too.

EIGHT

FINN

I whistled as we strolled from Maik's to the nearest taxi rank several blocks away.

Tonight had turned out better than I expected. Not only had Ellie preserved my crown jewels by not kneeing me for getting her to the bar under false pretenses, she'd stayed and we'd had a great dinner.

Though it wasn't the soft shell crab, coriander prawns, slow-cooked veal, hickory-smoked trout, pork belly in black vinegar, and thyme-infused peach sorbet that made the evening great so much as the way she'd unwound. For the first time in a week, I'd glimpsed the woman behind the crimson lipstick and gelled hair and overly made-up eyes.

Ellie loved junk food and old action movies and drinking coffee at Circular Quay on a Monday morning. She hated sports and politics and moths. And she adored city life in Sydney.

She'd been so animated at one point, she'd started spouting facts about the Cross like an encyclopedia and while I hadn't been particularly interested in learning the El Alamein Fountain's dandelion design done by a New Zealand architect had been copied around the world, I was riveted to her every word because she'd come alive.

Who knew the silent, truculent woman of the past week loved to talk, and our six courses flew by. During each and every one, I found myself falling under her spell.

What made Ellie more alluring was the fact she had no idea how goddamn gorgeous she was. Strip away the black leather and the plain singlet tops, the make-up and the chunky jewelry, and the invisible armor that she wore with pride, and Ellie was beautiful on the inside.

I wished I could articulate half of what I was feeling as we walked side by side, so I settled for entwining my fingers with hers instead.

She didn't pull away. In fact, she sidled closer, her hip bumping mine, making me a little crazy. Because while I'd been enthralled by her chatty side over dinner, it didn't stop me wanting to take her up against the nearest wall.

"What are you thinking?" she asked, glancing at me from the corner of her eye.

"You don't want to know," I said, my grip inadvertently tightening on her hand and she yelped.

"Sorry." I eased back on the grip and held her hand up, running my thumb over the thick silver band she wore on the middle finger of her left hand. "Did you know this design looks Celtic?"

"Hmm," she mumbled and removed her hand quickly, like she didn't want me studying the ring any closer. Interesting.

"You always wear it. Sentimental value?"

She gnawed on her bottom lip and damned if I didn't get a boner that made me lightheaded, that much blood drained south.

"Something like that," she said, looking increasingly uncomfortable.

"From an old boyfriend?" I persisted, needing to distract myself from the increasing urge to push up against her and let her feel exactly what affect she had on me.

"To forget an old boyfriend," she muttered, shaking her head, sadness down-turning her mouth as I inwardly cursed for putting a dampener on this evening when things had been going so well.

Needing to get us back onto more stable ground, I captured her chin in my hand and raised it, so she had no option but to look at me. "I can think of better ways to help you forget."

My implication clear, she stared at me for an eternity, her expression unreadable in the darkness cast by the alley behind me.

When the silence reached uncomfortable, she did the unthinkable.

Splayed both palms on my chest.

Pushed me backwards.

Slammed her mouth on mine.

My back hit the wall but the pain ricocheting down my spine was quickly replaced by a fireball of lust so swift, so overpowering, I almost staggered.

My hands spanned her waist and held her tight as we kissed like two people who hadn't done this in a long time. Passionate. Desperate. Frantic. Her pelvis grinding against mine. My cock straining. My balls aching for release.

She hooked a leg around my waist and I slid my hand between us. Wished she didn't wear leather. Because as I pressed against her clit through the layers, she growled, a purely primitive sound that made me want to fuck her right here, right now.

Wrenching my mouth from hers was the hardest thing I'd ever done. "Need to get home. Now."

As the madness of the moment passed, I expected her to pass off what had just happened as an aberration, something that could never happen again.

To my immense relief, she nodded. "Let's go."

I didn't need to be asked twice.

NINE

ELLIE

The taxi ride home should've sobered me up.

Not that I was drunk as such, because we'd been at Maik's for hours and I'd topped up my earlier beer buzz with a single glass of wine while stuffing my face with the divine food. So technically, I had no excuse for my behavior; first at the restaurant and later in the alley.

Finn was such good company and so easy to talk to I'd found myself blabbing. Telling him little things about myself. Small talk mostly but enough that we'd connected. And he'd listened, appearing enraptured by every stupid word that babbled out of my mouth. Heady stuff for a loner like me, having a sweet guy actually interested in hearing me out.

As for the way I'd jumped him in that alley...I had another two minutes to come to my senses. Change my mind. List every logical reason why we shouldn't have wild, climb-the-walls sex.

But as I locked the back door behind us and reset the alarm, I couldn't think of any.

"Go on. Get it out of your system." Finn trailed a fingertip down my cheek. "Tell me why we shouldn't sleep together."

Unnerved that he could read me so easily, I aimed for levity. "Who said anything about sleep?"

He smiled, the dim hall-light illuminating his teeth. "That's my girl."

Three words to rattle my common sense into reawakening.

I could never be his girl, his or any other guy's. Relationships built expectations and needs, and if those needs couldn't be met...I'd end up alone and shattered. Again.

"I'm not your girl."

I squared my shoulders and dragged in a deep breath. "I'm ten years older than you. I have no interest in anything beyond a one-night stand. And I don't want to discuss this tomorrow. Capish?"

"You're bossy." His fingertip trailed from my cheek to my jawline to the dip between my collarbones. "It's a big turn on."

I rolled my eyes. "Like you need the encouragement. You're just a walking hormone at your age."

Disappointment downturned his mouth as his hand fell away and irrationally I missed his touch. "I've had sex with two women in my life. Lost my virginity at nineteen, then had a relationship with the girl next door for three years."

He dragged a hand through his mussed hair, frustration lacing every word. "It'd be nice if for one second you'd believe I'm not some bullshitting guy out to score while I'm in town. That I think you're incredible. The most incredible woman I've ever met. And that you'd forget about the age difference because it's not relevant when two people share the connection we do."

I stared at him in open-mouthed shock. No guy I'd been with had ever been so blunt, so articulate. It made me flounder even more.

"Dammit, Ellie, I care about you. Why can't you accept that?" He cupped my cheek and despite the urge to run, I finally gave in and rested against his hand.

"I'll try," I whispered, the admission wrenched from deep within, from a deliberately sheltered soul who had given up believing anything that came out of a guy's mouth a long time ago.

He studied me, nerve-rackingly somber. What seemed like an eternity later, he said, "Your place or mine?"

I laughed. At last, a question I could answer unequivocally. "Yours."

I may be willing to let Finn into my heart a tad tonight, but no way was he seeing the real me by entering my apartment.

"Then what are we waiting for?"

Ignoring my inner self-preservation cynic screaming that I was doing the wrong thing, I walked upstairs with Finn, hand in hand. Pausing to kiss on the middle step. On the landing. Outside his door. Until all I could think about was getting naked and sweaty and forgetting every logical reason why I shouldn't do this.

He opened the door to his room and we practically fell inside. Staggered to the bed. I tore his button down shirt open, enjoying the ping of plastic against the floorboards. Unfortunately, leather wasn't conducive to tearing and after several fumbled attempts at the zipper on my pants I stilled his hands.

"Let me."

To my amazement he blushed and sank onto the bed. Propped on his outstretched arms, he watched me with an intensity that made my skin pebble.

I shrugged out of my jacket and let it fall to the floor, enjoying his hungry gaze on my braless breasts. I peeled my cotton singlet overhead and flung it away, as he made a half-strangled sound. I unzipped and wriggled out of my pants, he murmured, "Fuck me..."

"I intend to," I said, unashamed to be standing before him in my black panties. Because I could handle the lust in his eyes, the burning need for sex. What I couldn't handle was the way he'd looked at me a few minutes ago, with tenderness, as he told me he cared.

I hooked my thumbs into the elastic of my panties. "Should I do the honors or you?"

"Come here." His command was gruff, hoarse, the deepening of his voice and his delicious accent sending a tingle down my spine and zeroing in between my legs.

I stepped forward and he surged toward me, burying his face where I wanted him most.

"I want to taste you," he said, easing my panties down my legs and off. "Spread your legs."

"You didn't say please."

I liked teasing him at a time like this. It surprised me, how comfortable I felt with Finn.

"Do it." He muttered his command through gritted teeth. "Please."

Considering how tortured he sounded, I took pity on him and took a step sideways with each leg. "Better?"

"Hell yeah." He licked me with a long, sure sweep of his tongue and I bucked against him as he flicked my clit.

"Oh yeah, just like that," I murmured, my fingers finding purchase in his hair as he tongued me repeatedly, my orgasm building far too quickly.

I wanted to prolong it but was powerless as the tip of his tongue circled my clit with just the right pressure, faster and faster until I climbed. Tensed. Shattered. Floated back down to earth as he guided me down onto the bed.

"You're so beautiful," he said, kneeling at my feet, his eyes devouring me, his fingertips skimming my skin. Dipping into the hollows. Tracing the bony bumps. Contouring the curves.

It felt divine, my skin alight with his leisurely exploration, my nerve endings tingling. But I wanted more.

"I want you inside me...oooh..." I ended on a moan as he captured a nipple in his mouth, laving it, nipping it, while pinching the other between his thumb and forefinger.

He raised his head to grin at me. "I do believe you omitted the magic word."

"Do me. Now." As he resumed sucking my nipple, the suction intensifying the throb between my legs, I all but yelled, "Please!"

"With pleasure." He pushed into a standing position and it was my turn to enjoy the show as he unbuckled, unzipped and stepped out of his jeans.

I zeroed in on the bulge in his boxers, my mouth dry as he took them off with an expression akin to bashful pride. And he had every reason to be proud, considering the length and thickness jutting toward me.

"Impressive," I said, beckoning him with a crooked finger. "So come impress me."

He laughed and I joined in, taken aback again by how

good this felt, how right. I never laughed during sex. I never felt this relaxed.

Very occasional sex took the edge off for me. A quick strip, a quick fuck, a quick exit. None of this...foreplay that extended beyond the physical and was so darn appealing.

"Seeing as you asked so nicely..." We grinned at each other, a couple of idiots, as he donned a condom from the bedside drawer. Watching him slide the latex on served to ratchet up my excitement and I squirmed with wanting him inside me.

He sat on the edge of the bed and hauled me onto his lap. Breasts to chest. Face to face. Intimate.

That's when it hit me, why this was so different from other sexual encounters.

The intimacy.

I didn't do intimacy. Not anymore. It frightened the crap out of me. Besides, it didn't make any sense. I'd known Finn a week. How could I feel so at ease with a guy I barely knew?

"You still with me?" His hands cupped my face, demanding I return to the moment and stay focused on what was important. The two of us slaking this undeniable thirst for each other.

"Does this answer your question?"

Bracing my hands on his shoulders, I lowered myself onto him. Inch by exquisite inch. The fullness making me gasp. Until I enclosed him.

He groaned, his hands sliding from my cheeks toward my breasts, where he kneaded as I started to ride him. I started slow but couldn't maintain the pace, the delicious friction of him filling me so completely making me crave more.

Sensing my need, his hands drifted from my breasts to my hips. Anchoring me. Guiding me.

Then he started to move, upward thrusts that made me cry out.

"You okay?"

"Never better," I ground out, my fingernails digging into his shoulders as he pumped upward. Harder. Faster. Urging me toward another climax.

He shifted slightly, changed the angle and I screamed as I came, my orgasm slamming into me so fast my head spun.

For some inexplicable reason, tears stung my eyes. Maybe too much pleasure did that to me, I was that unused to it.

As Finn yelled my name and I clung to him, I wondered if I'd ever be the same.

TEN

FINN

The view that greeted me when I stepped into the cellar was Ellie's cute arse in the air as she bent to check hoses.

After the week we'd had, where we'd spent every spare moment in my bed, my first instinct was to cross the short space between us, rip her panties off and bury myself between her legs.

She'd feel like heaven: hot, slick, tight. I couldn't get enough.

My cock hardened and I was grateful for the empty bar and locked doors

"Hey beautiful, need help with those kegs?"

She glanced over her shoulder, a sly grin alerting me to the fact she wouldn't be averse to me carrying out my lecherous thoughts.

"The kegs are fine but this?" She wiggled her arse. "May need some of your specialty TLC."

There was nothing tender, loving or caring in the way I was on her in a second, flipping her cotton skirt up—thank God she'd taken to wearing them after hours the last week—and unzipping my fly.

She bent over the stacked kegs further as I rolled a condom on, tore her panties aside and plunged into her, my mind momentarily blanking as it always did when I first slid home.

Then the sensations started to bombard me. Intense, indescribable pleasure. Being gripped by hot, tight velvet. Being milked. Being driven to the brink far too soon, wanting to hold back, to prolong, but powerless to do so.

Loud, slapping sounds mingled with her moans as I thrust into her. In and out. Totally consumed. Totally enclosed. Totally lost.

As her pants intensified, my balls tightened. Holding her hip with one hand, I slid the other around the front. Found her clit. Rubbed.

She came in an instant, her long, low moan raising the hairs on the back of my neck. I kept rubbing as I pumped into her, fucking so hard my cock felt like it exploded as I came.

I slumped over her, held her, until I could breathe again.

"I think I'm officially assigning you to cellar duties," she said, backing against me a little and I straightened, still holding her tight as I slid out of her and disposed of the condom.

"If I get to do that daily, you won't have to pay me."

"That sounds gross and tawdry." She snickered and turned in the circle of my arms, her nose a cute little wrinkle.

"You know what I mean." I slapped her arse and she

giggled, a lighthearted sound I'd come to hear more often over the last seven days.

Seven exquisite days when we'd worked and played together. Laughed together. Teased together. We'd grown closer and while I knew it couldn't last, I was determined to make the most of it.

"Shall we head upstairs?" She ground her pelvis against mine. I didn't need any encouragement.

"Sure, if we're all done here."

She slipped out of my arms, only to snag my hand. "Honey, we're just getting started."

"Another all-nighter, huh?" I pretended to stagger and clutch my back. "You're wearing me out."

"Bullshit." She winked. "There has to be some benefits to having a toy boy."

Loving how she never brought up our age difference anymore except in jest, I pointed at my groin. "You seem to enjoy the benefits of my toy just fine."

She rolled her eyes. "Don't go getting a big head."

"I thought you liked it that way." I placed her hand on my swelling cock to prove it.

"God..." She sighed, gave me a gentle squeeze, before half bounding-half sprinting up the stairs, stopping to crook her finger at me. "Hurry up."

I didn't have to be asked twice.

We'd reached the top step when a pounding sounded at the back door.

"Who the hell's that?" Whoever it was, I'd kill them for their lousy timing.

"Kye's the only one who'd use the back entrance after hours." She made a cute exasperated sound akin to a snort. "Think we can ignore it?"

The pounding increased as Ellie's mobile started blaring

its usual hard rock ringtone.

"Guess not." She looked as disappointed as I felt. "I'll go see what he wants."

"Let me go."

Because I knew for a fact guys talked less and that meant I could get rid of Kye faster.

She hesitated, then nodded. "Okay."

"Won't be long." I captured her face in my hands and kissed her. "Wait for me."

Her eyes widened, fear lurking in their indigo depths. Guess that answered any unasked questions I may irrationally contemplate about us being involved in any kind of relationship beyond casual. I'd meant wait for me in the bedroom but the way I'd said it had obviously triggered something for her. Looked like Ellie waited for no man.

"See you soon," she murmured, turning away, effectively shutting me down so I couldn't probe.

Torn between wanting to go after her and getting rid of Finn as fast as I go, I chose the latter. The mysterious Ellie and her secrets could wait until later.

Zipping up my fly, I headed for the back door. With my first day near-mugging fresh in my mind, I peered through the barred glass window before opening the door.

"Hey Kye, what's up?"

"I need a drink." He pushed his way past me and headed for the bar. By his wild-eyed expression, this could take a while. Damn.

I relocked the door and followed him. "What'll you have?"

He sneered. "I'll help myself."

I held up my hands in surrender and took a seat at the bar, wondering what had happened to make Kye this edgy. Maybe I should get Ellie after all.

"You want anything?" Kye held up a whiskey bottle after sloshing a double shot into his glass.

"No thanks."

"Suit yourself." He downed the drink in two gulps and topped up twice, finally recapping the bottle much to my relief.

A drunk Kye would have to stay overnight and for what I had planned with Ellie, I didn't want guests.

"Bad day?"

"The fucking worst," he said, sliding onto the bar stool next to me. "I lost it on the court."

When he turned his head to stare at me, I wished I'd had that shot of whiskey after all. Kye looked broken, like he'd done more than throw a hissy fit while playing tennis.

"Never done that..." He swirled his drink while staring into its depths. "Usually I burn off anger while I'm playing but today, I had a shitfit to end all shitfits."

"Why?"

He flinched, as if I'd physically flayed him. "The dickhead I was playing in an interclub match knew about my background. He started taunting me..." He downed his double shot and slammed the glass on the bar. "I've put up with worse but..."

I didn't know whether to leave well enough alone or if Kye wanted to talk more, but I'd never seen a guy look so damned defeated so I settled for some gentle prodding.

"But?"

He glanced up from his glass, the bleakness chilling his eyes making me want to turn up the heating. "He badmouthed Mum and I snapped."

"Understandable—"

"It's been five years since she died, you'd think I'd know better." His bitterness was audible. "I cleared the net, had him in a headlock and would've punched the shit out of him if my practice partner hadn't dragged me off."

"Don't beat yourself up. I'd do the same to anyone who badmouthed my mum."

For the first time since he'd stormed in, Kye's shoulders lost some of their tension. "I'd pay to see you rough up anything bigger than a mouse, Irish."

"You calling me a weakling?" I flexed an arm and pushed up my bicep with my free hand. "Because I could take you."

Objective achieved when Kye semi-smiled. "I'd like to see that."

We chuckled as I removed my fingers and my bicep returned to its usual leanness.

He glanced toward the back stairs and my heart sank. If he wanted to talk to Ellie, he could be here all night, and as unsympathetic as it seemed, I didn't want that. But the guy looked so lost, so bereft, I had to offer.

"Do you want to talk to Ellie?"

"Nah, I'm good." He pushed the empty glass toward me. "You'll do."

Somewhat relieved, and a little chuffed he valued me as enough of a friend to confide in, I grabbed the glass and placed it out of reach. "I'd make a lousy agony aunt but I'm willing to listen if you don't get shit-faced."

Kye grunted, rubbed a hand over his face. "I'm sick of talking about my fuck-ups. What's happening with you?"

I couldn't hide my goofy expression and Kye groaned. "Don't tell me. I can see it all over your dufus face."

"Ellie's the best," I said, wondering if it'd be worth running my crazy idea past Kye.

"You'll get no argument from me." Kye studied me. "What's going on? You look like a kid who's been given a pet lizard for Christmas and doesn't know what to do with it."

"I'm thinking of staying," I blurted out, knowing it sounded as ludicrous articulated as it did in my head.

"In Sydney?"

I nodded, suddenly glad Kye had dropped by unexpectedly. I'd been going nuts the last few days, ever since the thought had popped into my head that I wouldn't have to leave Ellie. Not if I didn't want to.

"But what about your turf management position in Melbourne?"

I shrugged. "Jobs come and go."

Kye's eyebrows rose. "You're serious?"

"Yeah."

"Shit, you're naive." Kye shook his head. "You're out of your mind to give up a solid future in your career field for a woman, even if Ellie is one of the best."

Stunned by Kye's vehemence, I tried to marshal a suitable response when he continued.

"Mate, let me give you some advice." He slapped me on the back. "Think with your big head, not your little one."

I shoved Kye away. "You're a fuckwit if you think this is just about sex."

"Whoa." Kye's audible admiration did little to quell my rising temper. "You've got it bad."

"I care about her," I murmured, my shoulders slumping as the fight drained out of me. "And I have no fucking clue how to convince her of that."

"Tell her," Kye said, surprisingly somber. "What have you got to lose?"

The way Ellie shied away from anything deep and meaningful?

Everything.

ELEVEN

ELLIE

I snuck a peek downstairs and when I saw Finn settle onto the barstool next to Kye, I knew he'd be a while.

Kye often did this; turned up at the bar at all hours if he'd had a bad day. Because the kid was so mixed up, he had a few of those. Usually we'd share a drink, shoot pool, play poker, talk. At least, Kye would talk, I'd listen. I didn't mind being his stand-in mum. He was a good guy and Sheree would've done the same for me if I'd had a kid.

An old, familiar pain twanged my chest at the thought of what I wanted and would never have. Now, like back then when my perfect life had crumbled before my blinkered eyes, I marched to my apartment, slammed the door and headed for the bedroom.

It took me a full five minutes to realize I was zipping into my leathers, gelling my hair, applying lashings of red lipstick and slipping on the chunkiest silver rings I could find, when I should've been getting ready for Finn.

"Jeez," I muttered, sinking onto the edge of my bed, letting the four-inch spiked heel boots in my hand fall to the floor.

I didn't have to run away anymore. I owned this place. This was my sanctuary. And I had the promise of all-night sensational sex to take the edge off my sorrow.

Because that's exactly how I felt every time I rehashed the past, even in my head. Sad. Bone-deep grief, the kind that could sap energy and render me useless if I let it. I should know. I'd let it get a grip on me for almost a month after Dougal had first left.

Dougal. The man of my dreams. My high school best friend who'd had enough of a bad boy edge to make him attractively dangerous, yet gentle and sweet around me. The guy who'd promised me the world. The guy who'd given me jack-shit instead.

Angry that I'd let my memories get the better of me, I stood and started ripping off my clothes, before heading to the bathroom to remove the rest of my mask. I didn't need war-paint or fierce hair to be with Finn. And that's what I needed right now: to be with Finn.

Finn made me feel good. Made me feel hopeful. Made me forget.

I showered quickly and donned a robe. I opened my door, heard the murmur of voices at the back door and padded barefoot to his room. I'd slipped under the covers as Finn's footsteps pounded up the stairs.

The bedroom door flung open and I startled. Finn stalked into the room, auburn curls awry, aquamarine eyes glowing with fervor.

"Is everything okay—"

"Yeah, Kye's good, he just left." He stared at me for an eternity, before closing the door.

"I need you to listen." He made a zipping motion over his lips as he strode to the bed and sat next to me. "Hear me out without saying a word."

"O-kay..."

I didn't like his expression, halfway between bold and batty.

He grabbed my hand, intertwining our fingers. "I've been thinking about this for a week."

Not liking the sliver of foreboding shimmying down my spine, I eased back a little. "About what?"

"Staying. In Sydney."

Three little words to strike fear into my heart when I had to believe that what we had was sex and nothing more.

While I was freaking out on the inside, I tried to appear calm and clarify, because Finn could be sticking around for a variety of reasons.

I willed my voice to remain steady. "Why?"

His eyebrows shot up. "You seriously have to ask?"

He squeezed my hand. "I care about you. A lot. And I thought—"

"Stop." I yanked my hand out of his and scooted across the bed, away from him and out of reach. "This is ridiculous."

Confusion creased his brow. "I don't understand—"

"That's obvious."

I reached for my robe draped on the end of the bed and shrugged into it. No way could I have this conversation naked. Not when I'd need to storm out of this room shortly before I relented and listened to the nagging voice inside my head that insisted I knew exactly where this was going but was too damn scared to admit it. "Look, Finn, we've had fun but you can't stay in Sydney because of me."

His mouth flat-lined, his glower mutinous. "The connection we share is more than sex and you know it."

Hugging my knees to my chest, I shook my head. "What I know is you've got your whole life in front of you. A career to forge. Women to meet. Kids to raise."

I waved my arm around the room. "That's not going to happen if you're stuck in a shithole tending bar because you've left Ireland for the first time and have confused a good fuck for something more."

I hated cheapening what we'd shared, but I had to do it. Had to belittle and taint our relationship so he wouldn't make the biggest mistake of his life.

Because of me.

Rather than erupt and tell me to get the hell out, his eyes narrowed, his stare too astute, too assessing. "Tell me who hurt you so badly—"

"I'm done here."

I swung my legs over the end of the bed and tried to stand as he lunged across and hauled me back with an arm around my waist.

"You're pushing me away verbally, just like you do everyone else with your bad-arse attitude and leathers and make-up." He tried to hold me tighter and I wriggled, desperate to escape. "Stop the pretense because I can see right through your armor." He murmured in my ear, "I'm not leaving, Ellie, so get used to it."

I stilled, the fight draining out of me, replaced by a fierce desperation to do the right thing. Because for one terrifying second, I wanted to believe. Believe that Finn really could see through me, and that he liked me anyway, that he'd stay regardless.

That he'd never run.

But that second passed and the reality was, I'd have to push him away, once and for all.

To do that, I'd have to lay myself bare and tell him the truth.

"Let me go," I hissed through clenched teeth, elbowing him at the same time. I made contact with his solar plexus and he released me on a loud exhalation.

I stood, spun around to face him. "If you stay, what do you envisage happening with us? White picket fence? Housewife? A family?"

He eyed me warily. "You know that's what I want eventually, but our relationship is new and—"

"There is no relationship," I yelled, making us both jump. "You'll head to Melbourne to complete the internship your grandfather bent over backwards to get. You'll meet some sweet girl who'll give you the seven kids so you can replicate your parents. And you'll forget all about the fling you had at the first stop of your Aussie adventure."

"I won't forget." He stood so quickly I stumbled trying to back away. "And just because I opened up to you about wanting a big family one day, don't use it as an excuse to push me away when we're only getting started."

He tried a lop-sided smile, the one that slam-dunked my heart every time. "Because I'd settle for three brats, you know. Maybe even two—"

"I can't have kids!" I screamed, my throat convulsing. "I'm a fucking decade older than you. And by some remote chance we could ever make a relationship work, I can't give you what you want..."

My chest heaved with the effort to subdue the sobs making breathing difficult. "I was like you once. Naive and hopeful, with big plans and big dreams. The perfect relationship with the perfect person, or so I thought. Then the going got tough. We found out I was reproductively challenged. And he didn't want me because I was flawed. So when your dreams turn to shit, the people around you run and the only one you can depend on is the last person standing."

I touched his shell-shocked face for the last time. "That person is me."

I angrily swiped at the tears trickling down my cheeks. "I choose *me*."

Then I walked away without looking back.

TWELVE

FINN

I went after Ellie.

Hammered on her door. Pounded on it until my fists hurt. Desperate to hold her, comfort her, love her.

Because if the pain ripping through my chest was any indication, I must love her. There was no other explanation.

Her pain was my pain and Ellie was hurting. Big time. The devastation contorting her beautiful face when she blurted the truth...I'd never seen anything like it. And it made me feel dumber than ever.

How many times over the last week had I rambled on about my family? Telling tales of Maeve and Ciara exploiting their identical twin status by playing pranks. Waxing lyrical about Connor, Liam, Aiden, and Sean, a dufus for idolizing my brothers but proud at the same time. Raving on about our close-knit loyalty, our celebrations, our togetherness. How much I wanted the same when I eventually settled down.

All the while, Ellie had nodded and appeared interested, when she must've been dying a little inside. By her impassioned, devastating outburst, I'd rubbed her face in the one thing she wanted most but couldn't have: kids.

I tried one last time, bashing at the door with my forearm. "Ellie, please. Let me in. I want—"

"Fuck off," she yelled, followed by the sound of something crashing against the door and shattering.

Wincing, I backed away from the door. She needed space, I'd give it to her. So I trudged back to my room, sank onto the bed and stared at the ceiling. For an hour. Ellie's revelations and consequent freak-out reverberating through my head.

The thing was, as much as I loved my family and being surrounded by siblings, kids weren't a deal-breaker for me. Especially with the right woman. And I now knew that woman was Ellie.

I wanted to hang around, have a relationship, see if we really did fit before even contemplating anything serious yet she'd jumped straight to kids when I'd told her my plans.

Interesting.

It meant Ellie had been thinking ahead, way ahead, envisaging the two of us together, being totally committed. That told me more than her defensive behavior ever could.

She was invested in us already.

She could push me away all she liked but I wouldn't give up.

Not without a fight.

THIRTEEN

ELLIE

As I swept up the pieces of the glass I'd thrown at the door and tipped them into the bin, a shard pierced my thumb.

"Bloody typical," I muttered, sucking my thumb and glaring at the offending glass. Yeah, like it was a responsible for the total balls-up before.

Why the hell had I told Finn the truth? I could've pushed him away, fired him, made him leave, but the minute he'd started spouting all that romantic crap about staying around for me, I'd lost it. Completely.

Deep down, I knew why.

I yearned. Yearned to have what he had with his family. Yearned to have that closeness, that bond, that mayhem. The stories he'd told during our time together over the last week highlighted chaos, siblings that bickered and fought and teased, but siblings who would fight to the death to stand up for family.

It made me want kids all the more and I'd be lying to myself if I didn't admit to envisaging a bunch of tousled-auburn-haired brats with eyes as blue as their father's.

I was that far gone with Finn.

Finn, with his roguish smile and crinkly eyes and sex-me-up Irish accent.

Finn, who was ten frigging years younger than me though seemed more mature.

Finn, who made me laugh, who made me feel feminine, who made me...whole. Whole in a way I hadn't felt for a long time, not since I'd lived with Dougal in a picture-perfect three-bedroom brick cottage with a yard waiting to be filled with our ragamuffin kids.

Tears filled my eyes again and I reached for the nearest anesthetic: tequila, straight up.

Finn and I were over.

I'd get Kye to fire him and put him on a Melbourne-bound train or plane. That would be the end of it.

I sloshed a triple shot of tequila into a glass and slammed it down, straight. The alcohol scorched a trail from my throat to my gut, but it did little to burn away the pain making me clutch my chest.

Nothing would help ease that pain. I knew that first-hand. It took me a year to get over Dougal.

It would take an eternity to get over Finn.

In the meantime, I needed to feel nothing. Numb.

This time, I filled the glass to the brim.

FOURTEEN

FINN

When Ellie didn't answer her door the next morning, I contacted the one person who could help.

Kye answered on the first ring. "If you've broken her heart, I'll have to break you."

"More like she's broken mine," I said, rubbing the grit out of my eyes.

"She didn't take kindly to the news you're a love-struck schmuck?"

"You don't have to sound so bloody amused."

Kye's chuckles petered out. "Sorry, mate, it's not surprising Ellie shot you down. But don't give up. I've never seen her the way she is around you so she's doing her usual putting-up-barriers thing. She'll come around."

Hope made me sit a little straighter. "You think?"

"Absolutely. Where is she now?"

"Holed up in her room, not answering the door."

"At midday on a Sunday?" Kye tsk-tsked. "That's what she used to do when she first came to Sydney. Go on benders in her room, sleep 'til two."

"Shit," I muttered, feeling more of a bastard than I did last night. "What should I do?"

"As someone who was on the receiving end when Mum sent me round one arvo to wake Ellie up, trust me, you don't want to go there."

Great, so much for Kye helping me out. "I'm in love with her," I blurted, feeling like an idiot.

Guys didn't talk about this stuff but I had to do something proactive. I'd had enough of sitting around doing nothing. I'd been up the whole night, alternating between pacing and mulling and staring blindly at the hotchpotch crowd milling along Darlinghurst Road in the wee hours.

"Listen, meet me out the front in an hour. I'll help you find your balls." Kye sniggered. "Because the very fact you mentioned the L word to me suggests you're in way over your head, Irish."

"Okay," I said, and hung up.

Getting out of here for a while would do me good. Hopefully Kye would help me come up with a strategy to win Ellie over once and for all.

Though ninety minutes later, I questioned the wisdom of entrusting Kye to give me advice as I sat in a crowd of red and white-wearing fanatics at the Sydney Cricket Ground.

"Nothing like a good game of Aussie Rules footy to get the blood pumping," Kye said, handing me a beer in a plastic cup. "What do you think so far?"

"It's a poor imitation of Gaelic football," I said, sounding petulant and not caring. "Though I always root for the underdog so the fact the blue and white team, the

North Melbourne Kangaroos are thrashing the locals, is a good thing."

"Don't let anyone in this parochial crowd let you hear that." Kye pointed to the Swans emblem on his cap. "Sydney Swans rule."

"What are you, five?"

Kye raised his beer in a mock toast. "Come on, man, I'm trying to get your mind off things. Surround you in testosterone. Make sure you don't turn into a wuss."

"Just because I love Ellie doesn't make me any less manly."

"Just because I love Ellie..." Kye imitated in an exaggerated falsetto. "Heads up, Irish, talking mushy shit does make you sound less of a man."

I placed my plastic cup filled to the brim on the concrete under my chair. "Listen, this was a bad idea. I'm leaving—"

"I thought telling Ellie how you feel might make a difference." Kye shook his head. "Guess I was wrong."

I paused. "What do you mean?"

"Ellie's...flawed." Kye hesitated, downed the rest of his beer, before continuing. "I've known her a long time and she's buttoned up tighter than a nun's habit. She won't let anyone in. She doesn't trust easily."

He poked me in the chest. "So if you told her how you feel and she still shut you out? I don't think you've got a hope in Hades."

But I did have a hope.

If what Kye had just said was true, Ellie didn't trust anyone. So why did she trust me with the truth?

"You don't know anything about her past?"

Kye shook his head. "Don't think she told Mum either.

She just arrived one day, they became friends and Ellie became a Kings Cross fixture."

That sealed it. If I was the only one she'd told about not being able to have kids and her guy running out on her because of it, she did feel something for me. And she'd used the truth to push me away before I got any closer.

For the first time since last night's confrontation, I felt like punching the air in victory.

We weren't over and I knew just what I had to do to convince Ellie of that.

FIFTEEN

ELLIE

Sunday had officially sucked: waking at two in the afternoon with a monster hangover, sneaking around to avoid Finn only to find him gone, Kye ignoring my frantic texts to sack Finn, and ending with me booking into a cheap motel on the outskirts of the city to avoid Finn until I could get Kye to do my dirty work.

Considering I still couldn't get hold of Kye, Monday wasn't shaping up any better.

My second double latte of the morning did little to wake me as I perched on my favorite bench at Circular Quay, watching the ferries. This was my ritual, a calming start to the week that never failed to quell the jaded cynic in me and resurrect the hidden optimist.

Because every Monday when I came to watch the busy harbor, I remembered doing a similar thing with my parents. Sitting by the manmade lake in Dubbo every week, watching the sailboats. It had been the rare time my parents were happy. Almost carefree. Buying me ice creams. Smiling at each other. Occasionally holding hands. Before Mum got bored and ran off with a younger guy, leaving Dad heartbroken and morose and disinterested in parenting his only child.

I'd hated Mum for her selfishness. Blamed her for my lack of siblings and lost family. It was the reason I'd wanted to have kids early, to make my own family.

Look how that had turned out.

But I returned to Circular Quay every Monday morning to remember a time I was happy, before family bust-ups and relationship failings and having my heart ripped out because I couldn't have what I wanted most.

"Thought I might find you here."

My heart sank as Finn sat next to me: too close, too gorgeous, too much.

"Leave me alone," I growled, draining the last of my coffee and instantly craving another. Not that I really needed it, because the caffeine didn't give me half as much of a buzz as Finn's proximity.

"Can't do that," he said, resting his elbows on the back of the bench and stretching out his legs, looking like a carefree tourist lapping up the sun. "We need to talk."

"No, we don't." I crushed the plastic cup in my hand and lobbed it into a nearby bin. "And by the way, you're fired. So pack your things and get out before I return."

To my astonishment, he laughed. "You're not getting rid of me that easily."

"Would you prefer I take out a restraining order?" My tone was sickly sweet. "Bet that would go down a treat with Immigration and your working visa."

He didn't speak and when I shot him a sideways glance, rather than seeing panic, I glimpsed amusement.

"You'd do anything to get rid of me, huh?"

"Yep." If I nodded any harder my head would fall off.

"Too bad for you, because I'm not going anywhere." He swiveled to face me and his fingertip brushed my shoulder. I jumped at the surge that awakened my body far better than the two lattes. "You trusted me with the truth. Now it's time I trusted you."

Damn him for piquing my curiosity.

"I'll take your silence as approval to continue?" His mouth twisted into a wry grin and I had a hard time blocking out the vivid memories of how his mouth felt against mine. And lower.

Cursing my stupidity for wanting to hear what he had to say, I managed the briefest of nods.

"The turf position in Melbourne? My grandfather's dream, not mine." He huffed out a long sigh. "I'm the epitome of the good Irish son. Family comes first. Lived in Cork my whole life. Went into the patriarchal business. Had a staid relationship with the girl next door."

"I know all this," I muttered, on the verge of saying to hell with this and bolting. Nothing Finn could say or do would change facts: no way could we be a couple, ever.

"Let me finish." He cleared his throat. "Being the family's poster boy can become pretty bloody tiring, so I'm done. Time to live life on my terms."

He stared at me, beseeching me to understand, while I remained clueless.

"I don't see what you finding a pair of balls has anything to do with me."

His roguish smile alerted me to an incoming zinger.

"On the contrary, you seem to be very interested in my balls."

For the first time in twenty-four hours, I felt like laughing. But I didn't, because making light of this situation would do nothing to speed up the end goal: getting Finn to leave once and for all.

"Turf management was a stopgap for me. I can see that now." He reached for my hand and I snatched it away, folding my arms and tucking my hands against my sides. "Honestly? I don't know what the hell I want to do career-wise, but I'm damn sure who I want as my partner while I make important decisions, and that's you."

I hated how my heart leapt at his sincere declaration. "Important decisions like how many kids to have?"

He pinched the bridge of his nose. "I've never lied to you and I'm not about to start now. Yeah, I want kids. But don't you think we should have a real relationship first?"

"What's the point, when I can't give you what you want—"

"This is the point."

Before I could react he kissed me, hard and fast and frantic. I should push him away, I knew that, but for a few mindless moments I allowed myself to indulge in the firmness of his lips, the talent of his tongue, and the sensations that flooded my body whenever he did this.

Surprisingly, he broke the kiss before I did, holding me at arm's length, his breathing ragged. "Tell me you don't want this."

I had to lie. It was my only option. But I'd vowed to never be like my mum, who'd lived a lie before running away without a second thought.

"I don't want us to start a relationship that's doomed from the start." He opened his mouth to respond and I rushed on. "I don't want you to end up regretting our involvement or worse, resenting me."

"But you've told me the truth upfront so I know what I'm getting into," he said, willing me to believe with his persuasive tone. "Here are the facts. I'm staying in Sydney because of you. Not because I need a visa. Not because I want anything from you. But because I...care about you."

His quick look-away hinted at something more than caring and knowing he may feel the same way I did made this all the harder.

"My folks had a massive age gap, fifteen years, so mum got bored and ran away with a younger guy when I was little," I said, not surprised when his eyes widened. "I'm reluctant to let history repeat."

"But you wouldn't be running away from anything." He rubbed my upper arms and damned if I didn't sway toward him. "You'd be running toward something. Me."

He made it sound so simple, so logical. Yet so insane.

"Let me clue you in to what happens when a relationship implodes. My Dad was left a shattered man incapable of making an emotional connection, let alone caring for his daughter. So I ended up wanting the one thing I didn't have, a family, and hooked up with the first guy who looked my way because of it."

The truth tumbled out of me in a rush and once I started I couldn't stop. "I moved in with Dougal the day I turned eighteen, in a perfect cottage we could barely afford. But I was starry-eyed and hopeful and in love. So in love I wanted to start a family ASAP to make up for the family I'd never had."

Finn's hands stilled, supporting my elbows, solid. I saw the surprise in his eyes. Wait until he heard the rest.

"He proposed a month later. I accepted. We wanted to

have our kids young and close together." I dragged in a breath, the pain of the past making my lungs seize. "When it didn't happen for us, we went through investigations. I discovered I was reproductively challenged and a month later Dougal left town."

Finn's fingers dug into me. "I'm so sorry—"

"That's the thing about being damaged. Doesn't make people want to stick around." I swallowed the lump in my throat. "First Mum did a runner, then Dougal bolted, so I left my picket fence dreams behind, moved to the Cross, toughened up and discovered it's much easier depending on myself."

"You're not damaged." Sorrow darkened his eyes to the deepest green as he cupped my face. "You've put your faith in the wrong people. Let me be part of your life, Ellie. I promise I won't let you down."

"Don't make promises you can't keep," I muttered, looking over his shoulder so I wouldn't be tempted to drown in his eyes, eyes filled with sincerity. "Want to know why I chose the Cross to settle? Because it's real and in your face and brutally honest. It doesn't pretend to be something it's not. It lets me be the person I want to be."

He released me, stepped back and gestured at my outfit. "That's what the armor's all about, isn't it? The leather, the make-up, the chunky jewelry, it's a mask to help you blend in."

"So?"

"But don't you see, you're giving up on your dream?"

My lips compressed. "I'm running a successful bar in the toughest part of town. I'm living the dream."

"You're settling."

"Fuck you," I said, turning away, but he wouldn't let me, his hand landing on my shoulder to spin me back around.

"What's reproductively challenged anyway? Not impossible to have kids, right? Which means you're the one who's running, who's too damn scared to face the tough stuff to get what you want. You want kids? Then do something about it."

I shrugged off his hand and shoved him away, my latent anger sparking by the hint of truth in his too astute observation. "You volunteering? To go through endless rounds of jerking off into a cup, giving me hormone injections, coping with mood swings, hospital visits, probable miscarriages and the exorbitant cost?"

For the first time since I'd met him, Finn looked angry, genuinely angry. A deep frown slashed his brows, his neck muscles bulged and his fingers curled into fists.

"Didn't you hear a word I fucking said earlier? Of course I'm volunteering," he yelled, causing several passersby to glance our way. It didn't faze him. "I love you, for Chrissakes and I want to be with you for the long haul, good times and bad, whatever it takes."

Shock rendered me speechless as he started to pace, muttering under his breath. "Goddamn stubborn woman. Too independent for your own good. Why can't you accept the fact I'm crazy for you and won't run out 'til you kick me out on my arse?"

And for the first time since he'd found me here, I dared to believe.

Finn was right. I was scared. Terrified, in fact, of trying to have kids and failing. Or discovering it was too bloody hard and I wasn't up to the effort.

But here was a guy willing to try. A guy who loved me.

A guy I loved.

In the end, I guess it came down to that.

I loved Finn.

In a way I'd never loved anyone and if I headed down this tension-fraught road, I couldn't think of anyone else I'd rather have by my side.

With unfamiliar elation fizzing through my body, I stood and broached the short distance between us. "How about we trial a relationship first, then see if your swimmers and my eggs are compatible later on?"

His head jerked up, his stunned gaze searching my face for answers I was finally, *finally*, ready to give.

"You mean—"

"Come here, you big, Irish hunk." I grabbed him and kissed the life out of him, before coming up for air. "And by the way? I love you, too."

The sound of a Manly ferry horn drowned out his response. I didn't care. There'd be plenty of time for words later. Maybe a lifetime of Irish-accent-laced words if I was lucky.

EPILOGUE

Two years later...

FINN

"I'm worried about Kye." I wrapped my arm around Ellie as we watched our best friend annihilate an opponent under a blazing Sydney summer sun. While I loved living in this vibrant city, I'd never get used to the heat.

"Me too," Ellie said, staring at Kye refusing to shake his opponent's hand before slouching off to the sidelines to swipe a towel over his face. "I've never seen him this angry all the time. Has he said anything to you?"

"No. You?"

She shook her head, soft honey-brown waves caressing my shoulder. I may have fallen in love with a spiky-haired platinum blonde, but I liked this softer version of her just as much. "You two hang out together. Surely you've picked up a vibe, a clue to what's really bugging him, something?"

I snorted. "We're guys. We body surf at Bondi. Drink beer at the footy. D&Ms aren't a feature."

She elbowed me. "Ssh, he's coming this way."

We both stood and waited for Kye to reach us. If he'd looked angry on the court, where he'd wiped his opponent 6-0, 6-1, 6-0, he positively glowered now. Something was definitely wrong and if I hadn't been so manic over the last twelve months doing a part-time management course while working the bar, and supporting Ellie through our third attempt at IVF, I would've noticed sooner.

"Great game, mate." I stuck out my hand and Kye almost broke it, his grip too firm, as he grunted a greeting.

"You okay?" Ellie touched Kye's arm and he flinched.

"Hey." Seriously concerned, I removed my arm from Ellie's waist and took a step toward him. "Want to get a beer?"

Kye shook his head, and when he finally met my gaze, I almost recoiled. I'd never seen so much devastated resignation before.

"I'm on probation at the academy." Kye glared at us like we'd been the ones to do it. "Got into a fight with a junior dickhead."

I wanted to say he must've had a good reason but over the last twenty-four months I'd got to know the young Aussie pretty well, and in that time I'd seen Kye's resentment build. As if he was angry with the world and didn't know what to do about it.

"Anything we can do?" Ellie reached out to Kye again and this time, he let her hand linger on his shoulder a moment before stepping out of touch distance.

"Nah, I've just got to get my shit together," Kye said, looking like it'd take a year of therapy to shift the baggage he carried around. "Thanks for coming down to watch me today."

"Anytime." Ellie glanced at me and I nodded, hoping our news might brighten Kye's day.

Kye's eyes narrowed as he glanced between us. "What's going on with you two loved-up bozos?"

"We'd like you to be Harriet's mentor at her name day ceremony," Ellie said, her awed gaze meeting mine as I marveled for the umpteenth time at the life we'd created, a gorgeous one-month-old girl with my eyes and her mum's feistiness.

Kye's expression softened. "Thanks guys, I'd love to." But all too soon, the darkness clouded his eyes again. "You sure you want an angry prick like me though?"

"You're our best friend," Ellie said, standing on tiptoe to kiss his cheek. "And if it weren't for you dragging this Irish reprobate into my bar to save his cute arse two years ago, I wouldn't be this happy."

This time, it was my turn for a kiss. Smack on the mouth.

"Get a room," Kye muttered, but he actually grinned. "See you at the bar for drinks in an hour?"

I nodded. "Just in time for you to read Harriet a story before bed."

Kye rolled his eyes. "All that kid does is sleep and crap."

I elbowed him. "And you love her for it."

"Yeah, I do," Kye said, a faraway look in his eyes, and I was grateful our friend could at least find joy in our baby girl. "See you soon."

Ellie snuggled into me as we watched Kye walk away. "I'm still worried."

"Me too, but all we can do is be there for him." I slid an arm around her waist and hugged her tighter.

"He's on some weird self-destruction kick..." Ellie's concern echoed mine.

"Maybe we should get him to babysit Harriet more often? That girl's enough to melt any guy's heart."

Ellie glance up at me, radiating pure joy as she usually did at the mention of our precious girl. "How did I get so lucky?"

As I swooped in for a kiss, I said, "We got lucky, babe. Really lucky."

She smiled against my mouth. "Next you'll be telling me you've got a stack of four-leaf-clovers stashed away and a leprechaun at the end of a rainbow."

"My luck's right here," I said, hugging her tightly, and intending to never let go. "Let's go see our girl."

Ellie didn't have to be asked twice.

Keen to read Kye's story?

CROSSING THE LINE *is out now*.

Laying it all on the line for love…

I'm tired of being good.
Achieving geek status at college doesn't equate with fun. So when I head home to my dad's tennis academy in Santa Monica on spring break, I'm determined to be bad. And hot Aussie tennis star Kye Sheldon is just the guy to help me break all the rules.

However, Kye's troubled past continues to dog him and attending the Cresswell Tennis Academy is his last chance at the big time. He can't afford to screw up...by screwing me, the boss's daughter.

But our relationship is much more than a vacation fling. Will it be game, set, match, when the truth is revealed? Or will we have a real shot at love-all?

FREE BOOK AND MORE

SIGN UP TO NICOLA'S NEWSLETTER for a free book!

Read Nicola's newest feel-good romance **DID NOT FINISH**

Or her new gothics **THE RETREAT** and **THE HAVEN**

Try the **CARTWRIGHT BROTHERS** duo

FASCINATION

PERFECTION

The **WORKPLACE LIAISONS** duo

THE BOSS

THE CEO

Try the **BASHFUL BRIDES** series

NOT THE MARRYING KIND

NOT THE ROMANTIC KIND

NOT THE DARING KIND

NOT THE DATING KIND

The **CREATIVE IN LOVE** series

THE GRUMPY GUY

THE SHY GUY

THE GOOD GUY

Try the **BOMBSHELLS** series

BEFORE (FREE!)

BRASH

BLUSH

BOLD

BAD

BOMBSHELLS BOXED SET

The **WORLD APART** series

WALKING THE LINE (FREE!)

CROSSING THE LINE

TOWING THE LINE

BLURRING THE LINE

WORLD APART BOXED SET

The **HOT ISLAND NIGHTS** duo

WICKED NIGHTS

WANTON NIGHTS

The **BOLLYWOOD BILLIONAIRES** series

FAKING IT

MAKING IT

The **LOOKING FOR LOVE** series

LUCKY LOVE

CRAZY LOVE

SAPPHIRES ARE A GUY'S BEST FRIEND

THE SECOND CHANCE GUY

Check out Nicola's website for a full list of her books.

And read her other romances as Nikki North.

'MILLIONAIRE IN THE CITY' series.

LUCKY

COCKY

CRAZY

FANCY

FLIRTY

FOLLY

MADLY

Check out the **ESCAPE WITH ME** series.

DATE ME

LOVE ME

DARE ME

TRUST ME

FORGIVE ME

Try the **LAW BREAKER** series
THE DEAL MAKER
THE CONTRACT BREAKER

EXCERPT FROM CROSSING THE LINE

Read an excerpt from CROSSING THE LINE

MIA

"You should do him." My BFF Dani pointed to a six-four dork in a custom-made suit sucking up to my dad next to the trophy cabinet. "Big hands. Big feet."

I rolled my eyes. "You don't actually believe that crap, do you?"

Dani sniggered. "Considering the amount of first hand research I've done, I think I'm a fairly good judge."

I hated how Dani did that, perpetuating the slut label she'd copped at high school. Dani liked to date. A lot. That didn't equate to sleeping around. But the fact she was blonde, gorgeous and had a great rack meant jealous girls had been happy to spread rumors. What made me madder? Rather than defend herself, she played up to it.

"Why do you still do that when we left high school three years ago?"

She ignored my question and tapped my nose. "Almost forgot. Big nose equals big dick too."

As usual, I didn't push her on an issue she knew bugged the hell out of me. I swatted away her finger. "He's not my type."

"Is anyone your type?" She grabbed two champagne flutes from a passing waiter and handed me one. "You've been here an hour and I haven't seen you scope out a single guy."

No great surprise. I returned home to my dad's place, the legendary Cresswell Tennis Academy in Santa Monica, every spring break, and not once had I found a guy remotely 'scope-worthy'. Egotistical sport junkies weren't my thing.

"That's because I'm so damn happy to see you again." I slid my arm around her waist and hugged tight. "I've missed you, sweetie."

"You're such a sap," she said, returning my semi-hug before easing away to down her champagne. "Let's get drunk and pick up the cutest guys here for a night of raunchy fun."

Another thing that pissed me off about Dani. We hadn't seen each other since last spring break, and our first night together she'd rather hook up with some anonymous guy than hang out with me.

I would've preferred to stay in tonight, watching corny old DVDs and eating ice cream from the tub while we caught up on gossip. Instead, Dani had arrived at my villa an hour ago, demanding I attend this lame party my dad was throwing for the new academy peeps.

I hated my dad's parties at the academy. Wall to wall tennis jocks whose egos matched their oversized racket collection, my dad's boring friends, and the general hangers-on who thought my dad walked on water because he'd won a record number of Grand Slams. Minimal food, maximum alcohol and requisite fake schmoozing. Country club exclusivity with an overload of testosterone.

But I couldn't say no to Dani. She was the only thing I missed about Santa Monica—discounting Dad—and we could hang out at some boring party for a while before doing our catch up over a Cookies'n'Cream tub later.

"That's an oxymoron. Cute guys here and raunchy fun." I glanced around, not seeing a single guy I'd give my phone number to let alone allow to touch me.

Dani's wide-eyed fake innocence didn't fool me for a second. "You sure you're not still a virgin?"

I snorted. "You know I lost my virginity to Andy in high school."

I hadn't told her about the only other time I'd had sex, with one of my friends at DU. And that had only been in the last few months. Pitiful, considering I'd been at the University of Denver for the last few years.

"That pencil dick? Time to find yourself a real man."

I stifled a giggle at Dani's accurate assessment of Andy's appendage. "How did you know he was a pencil dick?"

Dani rolled her eyes. "Babe, I could tell you the size, girth and prowess of every dickwad's cock at Dumbass High."

And there she went again, pissing me off. I knew for a fact she didn't sleep around that much back then. Now? I wouldn't know. Sure, Dani was her usual joking self when we Skyped weekly and emailed a few times a month, but the truth was I had no idea what my best friend did with her spare time these days. And by her account, there was a lot of that.

Dani lived off her trust fund. She didn't work. She

didn't do charity. And she didn't let me into her life anymore. Not like she used to.

Everything changed when she backed out of college before we were due to start. She never told me why. Gave some lame-ass excuse about not being interested in going it alone when she had her family's money to live off. Which I didn't believe for a second, considering Dani was the most independent person I knew and couldn't wait to join me at DU.

But I hadn't pushed because my BFF had looked seriously fragile at the time, like a Santa Ana wind could blow her over with the faintest gust. The flu, she'd said. I'd been terrified it had been something more serious. So I gave her the space she'd requested to get her shit together and when she finally Skyped me three months later, the old Dani was back. Irreverent. Brash. Irrepressible.

I elbowed her. "If you slept with half the guys you say you have, you wouldn't be able to walk."

"Practice makes perfect." She winked and did a fair imitation of a wide-stance cowboy swagger.

I laughed and shook my head. "I've missed you."

"Same here, babe." She slung an arm around my shoulder. "But here's the deal. If you don't bag the hottest guy here tonight, I'm going to sign you up with every online dating site in Cali. And I'll use that pic of you with the mud mask that looked like you had shit smeared all over your face."

"Is that the best you can do?" My snooty glare failed when I chuckled.

She tapped her bottom lip, pretending to think. "If that doesn't do the trick, maybe I'll get my mom to tell your dad you're lonely and would appreciate a fix-up with one of his tennis protégés—"

"You wouldn't dare." Dani's mom was a shameless Hollywood socialite who made meddling in people's lives an art form. As for my dad, I'd already been subjected to his less than subtle matchmaking as a teenager, which is why Dani's threat held serious fear factor. If those two got together on my behalf? A nunnery would be the only place I could escape their machinations.

Dani's grin was positively evil. "Try me."

I crossed my arms and puffed out a huffy breath. "Fine. I'm going to find the guy least like a tennis jock and do him tonight."

Translated: I'd walk up to him, beg him to play along with me long enough to get my trouble-making BFF off my case, then escape to my villa on the pretext I was spending the night with him.

I'd deal with telling Dani the truth in the morning.

"That's my girl." Dani tweaked my nose, grabbed my shoulders and twirled me in a slow three-sixty. "See anyone you fancy?"

Yeah, Ryan Gosling on the DVD cover of his latest movie, but that was back in my villa and unless I played along I'd be stuck here with Dani doing this all night.

Increasingly tired of Dani's never-ending need to hang out with a guy to make a party complete, I glanced around at the requisite tennis jocks in immaculate sports jackets, chinos and polo shirts. They chugged bottles of water, trying to make a good impression on my dad, the coaches and the rest of the academy crew. A few had potential in the looks department but they'd be too scared of pissing off my dad to play along with my lame scheme. No way would they leave with me with my dad looking on, on the pretense of screwing me or not.

And that's when I saw him.

The perfect guy.

Well, not *the* perfect guy, but the guy I knew could come through for me tonight.

He stood in the far corner of the room, away from the crowd, partially hidden behind the pot-planted palms, strategically placed to offer some privacy for recalcitrant loners like him.

He wore a scowl along with dark denim, a blue sports jacket and a tight white T that even at this distance outlined a muscular chest. Brown hair. Chiseled jaw. Sexy mouth. Eye-catchingly gorgeous, if he ever stopped glowering.

"You found him?" Dani said, when she noticed I resisted further twirling.

"Yeah." I jerked my head toward the corner. "Him."

"Fuck," Dani murmured, staring at me with newfound admiration. "I like the way you think, babe. He's got sex god written all over him."

"And soon I'll be all over him," I said, injecting enough fake bravado to sound believable while thinking 'I wish'.

Because a small part of me did wish I had the guts to go after a guy like that. A guy who looked bad enough to help me break free of being good.

Maybe I should amend my plan from getting him to pretend to hang out with me to flirting relentlessly so we hung out for real?

How long since I'd had fun with a guy beyond study dates and coffee in the college cafeteria? My grades were good. My life was good. I was *good*. For once, I'd love to be bad.

"Go." Dani shoved me in the guy's direction. "Report back in the morning."

I wiggled my fingers in a saucy wave at Dani as I strode toward the guy, who'd just downed a soda in record time.

By the time I was half way across the crowded room, I saw him duck out onto the terrace, which wouldn't be opened until later in the evening.

So I did the only thing I could.

Took a short cut to the terrace and crossed my fingers I could pull this off.

KYE

The second I stepped into the function room at the Cresswell Tennis Academy, I couldn't breathe. A stifling combination of designer perfume, overcooked shrimp and jock testosterone hung in the air like a miasmic cloud. The kind of scene I despised.

I wanted to leave. Ditch this pansy-arse party and the pretentious stuffy tennis establishment, leave Santa Monica and head back to Sydney.

But I couldn't. That's the thing about final chances. Screw this up and I was in deep shit.

"Would you like a drink, Sir?"

Sir? Seriously? Even the staff in this joint acted like they had a pole stuck ten-feet up their arse.

I stared at the waiter, who looked roughly twenty-two like me, and automatically reached for a beer. A coldie would take the edge off.

A coldie would also make me crave another, then another, to help me forget every godforsaken reason I was stuck in this hellhole for the foreseeable future.

In the first wise decision I'd made in months, I chose a soft drink instead. I downed it in three gulps and set the glass on a nearby table. I should mingle. I should do a lot of things according to my dad: lose the temper and the attitude, don't waste my talent and don't screw up.

Guess I should be grateful he hadn't disowned me after I'd busted that dweeb's nose back in Sydney. But even though we'd only known about each other for the last seven years, Dad stuck by me. He understood why I slugged the prick. No one got to call my mum a hooker, among other things, and get away with it.

"Drink, Sir—"

"No." I didn't want a frigging drink. I wanted to get the hell out of here. "Thanks," I said, softening my tone when the waitress stared at me with genuine fear.

Looked like I was failing with the change of attitude already. Not wasting my talent? Remained to be seen.

I could hit a ball around a court. Very well, according to the top coaches in Australia. The thing was, they didn't understand why I played tennis. Ironic, that the very attitude they wanted drummed out of me was what drove me to smash the shit out of that furry green ball.

When I saw another waiter bearing down on me with a sushi platter, I headed for the nearest exit. A locked French door leading out onto a semi-dark terrace. Seclusion. Perfect.

I flicked the lock and stepped out onto the slate tiled terrace that overlooked the pristine grass courts. Ten in total, with another ten clay and ten indoor surfaced behind the clubhouse. I couldn't fault the facilities here. The rest? Remained to be seen.

I propped against the wall and stared at the first court, the one I'd toured earlier with Dirk Cresswell, the academy's CEO. Dirk may be legendary in American tennis circles, with his record Grand Slam wins and golden boy charm, but from the fifteen minutes he'd taken to show me around today, he seemed like a self-absorbed, pompous prick. Who I had to play nice with if I didn't want to be turfed out on my arse.

"Hey."

I turned toward the girl's voice as she stepped out of the shadows, not sure what annoyed me most. The intrusion or the way she sauntered toward me, all long legs and cocky smile.

She was just my type: tall, sexy brunette with enough hip sway to make a guy wonder what made her so confident, and bedroom eyes that hinted at sin.

Sadly, this devil had just landed in the City of Angels and sin was the last thing on my agenda.

"I'm not in the mood for company," I said, expecting her to head back inside.

She didn't falter as she strode toward me. "Too bad, because I needed some air and this terrace is big enough for the both of us."

I could've left but there was something in the way she was staring at me that had me intrigued: like she wanted me but wouldn't have a clue what to do if she got me.

"Mia." She stuck out her hand. "Pleased to meet you."

"Kye." I reluctantly shook her hand. "Wish I could say the same."

"You don't like girls?" She slid her hand out of mine, the insolent quirk of her lips making me want to do something I shouldn't. Like kiss the smirk off her smart mouth.

"Love women." I took a step back, staring at her feet and slowly sweeping upward in a deliberate perusal meant to make a point. I wanted to make her squirm. It backfired, as I noted red nail polish matching her towering shoes, slim ankles, long legs, tight black dress that ended mid-thigh and hugged her lean bod, and pert tits. The frigging dress had a front zipper that just begged to be undone. Beyond hot.

By the time I reached her face, she was blushing.

"So which am I?" She leaned forward, giving me a generous glimpse of cleavage. "Girl or woman?"

If I were in the mood to flirt, Mia would've been perfect. I knew her type in a heartbeat. Good girl wanting to dabble. Her country club folks were probably inside sipping martinis and kissing arse. And Mia wanted to flirt with the jocks for a night, without the pressure of having to put out. I'd love to see how far I could push her, call her bluff. Instead, I had to drive her away before I did something stupid.

I'd had these moods before. I was better off alone.

"Honestly?"

She nodded, so I gave it to her straight.

"You're a college girl on spring break looking for a little down and dirty fun. Your folks probably drive a SUV, have dinner at the country club every night and play piss-poor tennis here weekly."

I saw hurt flicker in her big, brown eyes. Good. The faster she left, the better. So I drove the boot in harder.

"You want to slum it for a while, have a little holiday fun. String some poor dumb-arse tennis rookie along before giving him a severe case of blue-balls."

I deliberately turned my back on her. "Maybe the Aussie accent fooled you into thinking I'm that dumb-arse? But sorry, kid, you're definitely a girl and I only fool around with women."

I hated myself for treating someone I'd only just met like this. Mia whoever-she-was didn't deserve it, but the blackness was crowding in and I needed to escape.

Spying steps leading onto the lower level, I headed in that direction.

"My mom died when I was little. My dad drives a

Mustang, drinks scotch and doesn't have to kiss anyone's ass."

I heard the hitch in her soft voice and it slayed me more than her admissions.

"Sure, I play *piss-poor* tennis, if that means I play badly. So I guess one out of four ain't bad." I heard the snap of her fingers. "Oh, and you were right about one thing. You're definitely a dumbass."

I should've kept walking. Headed straight for those steps without looking back. But the fact I'd misjudged her so badly stung real bad. Hadn't I busted that dickhead's nose in Sydney because he'd misjudged my mum? And me?

I'd put up with being misjudged my entire life: the poor kid from the Cross whose mum ran a strip joint. The kid who was probably a pimp. The kid who must do drugs because of where he lived.

I'd copped it all and hated every minute of it.

So why the hell had I just done the same to a woman I barely knew and who didn't deserve to bear the brunt of my foul mood?

I stopped and turned back to face her. "I'm sorry."

"Don't be." She waved away my apology. "You can't help being a dumbass. You were born that way."

I smiled. For the first time in a long time. "You're probably right."

"So what's with the mood?" She tilted her head to one side, studying me. "Because I know that wasn't all about me."

I shook my head. "You don't want to know."

"Maybe I do ..." She hesitated, uncertainty clouding her eyes, before she straightened her shoulders. "You were right about one thing. I am in college. And I am on spring break." She puffed out a long breath. "This is my first night back home and I had to attend this stupid party, when it's the last thing I felt like doing, so I guess that makes us kindred spirits in a way."

"You don't know the first thing about me—"

"Chill." She rolled her eyes. "All I meant was you look like you don't want to be here. I definitely don't want to be here." She gestured at the tennis courts. "So why don't we ditch this lame-ass party and take a walk out there?"

She'd articulated my plan, with one flaw. I still wanted to be alone.

"I don't think so—"

"Shut up." She slipped her hand into mine before I could blink. "Let's go."

She tugged on my hand as I stared at our linked hands in disbelief. I had two options. Yank my hand free, make a big deal of this by stomping away and run the risk of her running to her daddy, who was probably besties with Dirk Cresswell. Or suck it up and leave like I'd intended. With a hanger-on.

"If we don't make a run for it now, the rest of the party will spill out here soon and then we'll be trapped."

I frowned, nodded. "Fine."

Though it wasn't, because as I allowed Mia to lead me down the steps, I wondered why I was still holding her hand. And enjoying it.

READ THE REST NOW!

EXCERPT FROM TOWING THE LINE

Dani's story, out now!

I need a new start. Anonymity. In a country where no one will know me, and the havoc I create. Not all the rumors about me are true. But I made one mistake too many in LA and attending an Australian college for a few semesters is the perfect solution.

I plan on avoiding guys. But the part-time tutor and sexy Aussie artist Ashton? Has me re-evaluating the wisdom of being a reformed bad girl. Ash is aloof, dedicated, serious, and I must corrupt him. So I seduce him. Not expecting to fall in love for the first time. And the last.

Because Ash has high standards and when he learns the truth about me, he'll join the long list of people in my life pretending I don't exist.

DANI

"Where's Loverboy?"

Not that I really cared where Mia's boyfriend Kye was.

I was enjoying having my BFF all to myself for a few hours before I boarded a plane to Australia to start my new life.

"He'll be here soon," Mia said, shoving the half-empty pizza box in my direction. "Said he had to see a man about a dog."

I helped myself to another slice of pepperoni, even though I'd barely nibbled the first. "What the hell does that mean?"

Mia shrugged. "Who knows? I just nod and smile when he comes out with those indecipherable Aussie-isms." Her eyes lit up. "Besides, who cares when he's that cute?"

"Fair enough," I said, eternally grateful we could actually talk like this considering I'd recently fucked up majorly by coming onto Kye with the intention of deliberately hurting Mia.

I'd been acting like the attention-seeking idiot I was and thankfully, Mia and Kye had forgiven me.

I'd told Mia the truth. Well, most of it.

She knew about the baby, why I'd blown off college and why I'd spent the last three years drifting through a haze of partying to forget.

But she didn't know all of it.

Nobody did.

And I intended on keeping it that way.

Sensing my sudden reticence, Mia pushed her plate away and placed a hand on my arm. "You okay?"

I nodded, swallowing the unexpected lump of emotion in my throat. I never got sentimental. Ever. I'd given up being that vulnerable a long time ago. Because feelings led to pain and I never wanted to feel as bad as I did when that bitch of a nurse told me I'd 'lost' my baby.

Like I'd lose anything so precious.

"Guess the reality of leaving all this to attend college in

Melbourne for a while has finally hit home." I gestured at the lavish lounge in my parents' Beverly Hills mansion. "I mean, how will I live without the ten widescreens, daily fresh sushi and thousand-thread count toilet paper?"

Mia laughed. "I hear they have two-thousand thread count in Australia." She winked. "How do you think Aussie guys have such hot asses?"

I chuckled, relieved the urge to bawl had receded.

"Talking about me?" Kye Sheldon strode into the room. Tall, blue-eyed, broad-shouldered, he was seriously hot and only had eyes for Mia as he made a beeline for his girlfriend and laid a hot, open-mouthed kiss on her right in front of me.

"Get a room," I muttered, actually enjoying the sight of my best friend being cherished in the way she deserved.

And Mia did deserve it. She'd always been good and why she'd hung out with me for the last fifteen years was beyond me. She was loyal, sweet and trusting. My voice of reason, I'd always called her. Which is why I hadn't told her about the baby.

Because when it came down to it, when I'd fallen pregnant at eighteen, I hadn't wanted to hear all the logical reasons why I shouldn't keep the baby. For the first time in my life, I would've had someone in my life to love me unconditionally. Someone to depend on me. Someone whose world revolved around me.

I'd never had that before. My parents pretended like their only child didn't exist. Too busy living an A-list Hollywood lifestyle in their suck-up job as agents to the stars.

Friends? Non-existent, discounting Mia, who had lived next door until her dad quit professional tennis to open his teaching academy in Santa Monica, and they'd moved. Mia had been my rock for so long. And I'd almost lost her through my own stupidity.

It had been the wake-up call I'd needed.

Time to stop drifting through life filled with self-pity. Time to make a new start. Time to start living again.

"Sorry," Kye drawled, not sounding sorry in the least as he sat next to Mia, his arm draped across her shoulders as she snuggled into him. "So Dani, ready to find a hot Aussie of your own Down Under?" He smirked. "Guys in Melbourne won't know what hits them when they get a squiz at you."

"Squiz?" I wrinkled my nose. "I'm hoping that's a good thing."

He chuckled. "Means a look at you."

Mia tweaked his nose. "Isn't he adorable?"

I rolled my eyes. "You two are pathetic."

"It's luuuurv," Kye said, holding Mia tighter. "So how about it? Ready to take Melbourne by storm?"

"Academically, maybe." Because that was my number one priority. To make the most of the six months exchange program I'd been offered at the prestigious Melbourne University and start an Arts major. Thanks to Kye's dad pulling strings at the university, I had a chance at a new life. I wouldn't screw it up this time. "I can't thank your dad enough for this opportunity."

"He's the best." The visible pride in Kye's eyes made me well up again. Wish I had parents who cared enough about me to want to help my friends. "If you need anything while you're in Oz, don't hesitate to ring him."

I nodded. "That's what he told me when I Skyped him to say thanks for doing all this."

"He's a good guy." Kye's grin alerted me to another of his typical teasing barbs. "Speaking of guys—"

"Not interested." I held up my hand. "Even if you're personally acquainted with Jesse Spencer, Josh Helman and Ryan Kwanten, I don't care." I placed a hand over my heart. "I'm swearing off guys, even hot Aussie ones, for the next six months."

Mia gazed adoringly at Kye. "Never say never, sweetie." She pecked Kye on the cheek. "Trust me, there's something about Aussie guys that is irresistible."

"I'll take your word for it," I said, meaning it.

I'd spent the last three years hanging out with the wrong guys, sleeping with some of them, getting wasted, doing whatever it took to forget my fucked up life.

The next six months in Australia? My own personal detox program.

No partying, no drinking, no drugs and no men.

Mia, ever perceptive, must've picked up on something in my expression, because she turned to Kye and said, "I'd love an orange soda."

"Coming right up." He stood and glanced at me. "Anything for you, Dani?"

I shook my head. "No thanks, I'm fine."

Biggest lie ever.

"No worries, back in a sec." He strolled toward the monstrous kitchen that included a breakfast nook complete with the latest video game consoles my dad loved. Kye would be a while. Last time he'd been here and volunteered to get us sodas, we'd found him playing some warrior shoot-out game an hour later.

The moment he left the room, Mia fixed me with a narrow-eyed stare. "You're in a funk and it's more than just living overseas for six months."

I sighed, wishing I could fob her off, but so tired of living a lie let alone telling another. "I'm terrified that even after doing all this, nothing will change and I'll still be the same screwed-up little girl screaming for attention."

Voicing my greatest fear didn't make me feel better. It made me feel sick to my stomach.

Because it was true. What if after all this I couldn't change? I couldn't forget? I couldn't learn to live with the mistakes of my past?

"Oh honey." Mia leaped off the sofa to come sit beside me on the floor. "You're the bravest person I know."

She took both my hands and wouldn't let go when I tried to extricate them. "It takes real guts to do what you're doing. Moving halfway across the world, making a start on a college degree, changing your lifestyle."

She squeezed my hands. "You've been through hell and you've made it through. This is your chance. And I have no doubt whatsoever you'll make the most of every exciting new minute."

"Will you be resurrecting your old pom-poms to go with that cheerleading routine?"

She laughed at my droll response. "You're going to be fine. Better than fine." She released my hands to pull me into a hug. "You're going to kick some serious Aussie ass."

Wish I had half her confidence because the way I was feeling now? Like I was standing on a precipice, about to go over the edge, with no safety net in sight.

ASHTON

I knew Mum was having a bad day the moment I neared her room and heard her grunts of frustration.

She'd always loved crossword puzzles but the more her brain deteriorated, the harder it became for her to do the simplest tasks, let alone find a three letter word for an Australian native bird.

I'd almost reached the end of the long corridor when a nurse laid a hand on my shoulder.

"Got a minute, Ashton?"

I stopped, turned and held my breath. Whenever one of the nurses wanted to talk before I visited Mum, it wasn't good.

"Hey Pam. How are you?"

"Good, thanks." The fifty-something redhead had the kindest eyes I'd ever seen. Pale blue eyes that were currently filled with concern. "But I wanted to have a quick word with you today."

The inevitable tension built in my temples and I quashed the urge to rub them. "Mum's okay?"

A pointless, dumb-arse question, considering Mum hadn't been okay in a long time. Not since I'd checked her into this special accommodation home two years earlier because it had become untenable to care for her at home.

The official diagnosis? Early onset dementia courtesy of a long-term alcohol abuse problem.

My diagnosis? She'd partied too hard, done too many drugs and drunk her life into oblivion to obscure whatever demons dogged her as a washed-up B-grade actress.

I resented her lifestyle. I resented every shitty thing that resulted in her being here at the age of sixty-three.

"Judy had a rough night." Pam hesitated, before fixing me with a pitying stare. "She may not know you today."

Fuck.

We'd reached this stage already?

I'd been warned there'd be more days like this. That as the dementia progressed, Mum's memory would deteriorate to the point she'd consider me a stranger.

I hadn't expected it to happen so soon and no way in hell I was prepared to handle it.

"Okay, thanks," I said, hoping Pam didn't hear the hitch in my voice.

Not for the first time since Mum had been diagnosed, I wanted to crumple in a heap on the floor and cry like a baby. But considering I'd been the only man in this family for a long time, losing my shit wasn't an option.

I had to stand tall and do what had to be done. And that included ensuring I made enough money to pay for Mum's bills. Something that was becoming increasingly difficult to do as my commissions dried up.

I needed to keep painting. I needed to keep tutoring at the university. And I needed to stop feeling like I was an automaton, oblivious to everything but getting through each day.

It was affecting my art, this emptiness inside me. But I needed to quash emotions and stay cold inside because if I started to feel again, I'd break down for sure.

Despite her lifestyle and her failings, Mum had always done right by me. I had to do the same for her.

"You're a good son." Pam squeezed my arm. "Come find me later if you have any questions or just want to talk, okay?"

"Thanks."

I knew I wouldn't take Pam up on her offer. I could barely hold my shit together when I left here after my bi-weekly visits. No way could I face Pam's kindness, especially if Mum was as bad as expected today.

I took several deep breaths to clear the buzzing in my head and waited until I could muster a halfway normal expression, before knocking on Mum's door and entering.

"How's the crossword coming along?"

My heart twisted as her head lifted and our gazes locked. Mine deliberately upbeat. Hers eerily blank.

"Who the fuck are you?"

And with those five words, I almost lost it.

My hands shook so I stuffed them into my jacket pockets as I cautiously crossed the room to sit in an armchair opposite hers.

Keep it simple, the nurses had warned if this happened. Don't startle her or press her to remember. Be casual. As for the swearing, aggression was a common reaction in progressive dementia. But to hear the F bomb tumble from Mum's lips was as foreign to me as seeing her sitting in a pink toweling bathrobe at five in the afternoon.

She'd always been glamorous, dressed to the nines with perfect make-up from the time she rose to the time she came home from whatever party she'd attended. Even as a kid, I had memories of Mum's vivid red lipstick and strawberry-scented shampoo as she kissed me goodbye before heading to an audition, her high heels clacking on our wooden floorboards as she left me in the care of the teenager next door.

That glamorous woman was nowhere to be seen now. Her blonde hair had faded to a washed out yellowy-grey. Her brown eyes were ringed with lines and underscored by dark circles. Her shoulders were shrunken, her back curved, her muscles flaccid from lack of use.

My beautiful, exceptional mother was broken. An empty shell.

And it killed me a little bit more every time I visited.

"I'm Ashton," I said, wishing I could elaborate, wishing I could yell, 'I'm your son. The one who wiped the vomit off your face more times than I can count. Who found you passed out on the floor and carried you to bed countless times over the years. Who would do anything to have you back.'

But I said none of those things. Instead, I swallowed my resentment—at the lifestyle that had put her here—and forced a smile. "I see you're a fan of crosswords."

"Stupid bloody things." She picked up the pen she'd discarded and tapped it against the magazine. "Can you think of a five letter word for a boy's building toy?"

"Block," I said, remembering the toy sets she used to buy me when she scored a role.

I'd treasured every single one, taking my time constructing the blocks into elaborate houses or fire-stations or castles, knowing it could be a long time between jobs for Mum.

Not that she didn't try hard but she never quite cracked it for a starring role. She'd got by with TV commercials and bit parts in anything from soap operas to local feature films.

Having me at forty had changed her life.

Roles were scarce for aging actresses, especially pregnant ones. I often wondered if that had been the start of her downward spiral. If she blamed me for ruining her life.

If she did, she never showed it. Mum adored me, loving me to the point of smothering. And even as she deteriorated, partying harder to forget the fact she wasn't working much, I always came home to dinner on the table.

"Thanks." She scrawled the letters into the boxes, her hand shaky. "Could you help me do the rest?"

"Sure," I said, taking care not to startle her as I cautiously edged my chair next to hers. "I like crosswords."

Knowing I was pushing my luck, I added, "I used to do them with my Mum."

I waited, held my breath, hoping for some sign she knew who I was.

"She must be a lucky lady to have a son like you," she said, her smile wobbly as she glanced at me with those blank eyes that broke my heart.

"I'm the lucky one," I said, as I settled in to spend some time with my Mum, hoping I had the strength to do this.

Because the way I was feeling now? As brittle as tinder-dry bark, ready to snap and fly away on the slightest breeze.

I had to be stronger. Strong enough for the both of us.

READ THE REST NOW!

EXCERPT FROM BLURRING THE LINE

Annabelle's story.

Annabelle Cleary travels half way around the world...to fall in love with the boy next door all over again.

Completing her degree at a college in Denver may just be the most exciting thing this small town girl has ever done. Until she discovers her new mentor is Joel Goodes, the guy who once rocked her world.

Joel isn't a keeper. He'll break her heart again. But Annabelle can't resist the sexy Aussie at his devastating best and soon they're indulging in an all-too-brief fling.

Annabelle wants it all: career, relationship and kids, in the hometown she's always loved. The same town that holds nothing but bad memories for Joel.

When they return to Australia, will it be a homecoming they'll never forget?

ANNABELLE

Being an Aussie studying in Denver was cool. Unless your BFFs were dating hot Aussie guys and never let up on your lack of a boyfriend.

"I don't get it." Mia handed me a champers, as I thanked the gods I'd had the smarts to come to the States in my final year of uni so I could drink legally at the ripe old age of twenty-two. "You've been here a year, Annabelle, and you haven't hooked up."

Dani snorted. "Not that I blame her. Half the guys on this campus have a pole stuck so far up their asses they can hardly walk."

"Maybe she's too picky?" Mia topped up Dani's glass. "She needs to lighten up."

Dani sniggered. "And get laid."

I sipped at my champagne, content to let Mia and Dani debate my lack of male companionship. They'd been doing it the last three weeks, ever since opening night of Ashton's first art show.

Dani never shut up about Ashton, her sensitive-soul artist boyfriend. The fact she'd met him in Melbourne, while staying in my flat, kinda irked a little. During my three years doing a bachelor's degree in physiotherapy at Melbourne Uni, I'd never met a single guy I'd drool over the way Dani did with Ash.

As for Mia, she was just as pathetic with Kye, her sexy tennis jock boyfriend. With both guys being Aussie, it merely exacerbated Mia and Dani's relentless assessment of my less than stellar love life.

"How do you know I haven't hooked up or gotten laid?"

Mia clinked her glass with mine. "Because, dear friend, all you ever do is study. You don't date. You don't party."

"And you don't even consider Mia's fix-ups," Dani said, raising her glass. "Or so I've been told."

"How can I put this politely?" I finished my champers in three gulps before glaring at them. "Piss off."

Dani laughed. "I know for a fact that's the Aussie version of fuck off."

Some of the mischief faded from Mia's eyes. "You know we're only teasing?"

I nodded. "Yeah, but since the arrival of this one—" I pointed at Dani, "—you haven't let up."

Mia made a zipping motion over her lips at Dani, who was the more relentless of the two. "That's because we want you to be happy."

"I am." The quick response sounded hollow even to my ears.

Because the truth was, I wasn't happy. Sure, my studies were going great and I'd made a bunch of new friends while in Denver. But I missed Melbourne. And on a deeper level, I missed Uppity-Doo, the small country town in northern Victoria I called home.

If I was completely honest, the last time I'd been truly happy was back there, in my final year of high school, when the guy I'd adored had reciprocated my feelings on that one, fateful night I hadn't been able to forgot. Several years and a trip across the Pacific hadn't dimmed the memory. Sadly, no guy had come close to eliciting the same spark.

"Sure you are," Dani said. "You could almost convince us looking like this—" She pulled a face with downturned mouth and deep frown, "—translates to happiness in Australia." She rolled her eyes. "But I've lived there for the last twelve months, remember, and I happen to know that's bullshit."

Mia took the empty champagne glass out of my hand and draped an arm across my shoulders. "Listen, sweetie, we'll lay off if you promise to keep an open mind tonight."

"What's on tonight?" Like I had to ask. Yet another party where my well-meaning friends would try to foist some unsuspecting guy on me. A guy I'd chat with and laugh with while pretending to enjoy myself, knowing by the end of the night I'd be heading back to my dorm alone.

I wasn't interested in transient flings. Never had been. And with an expiration date on my studies here in the States, it was the main reason I'd remained single by choice.

The other reason, where I was pathetically, ridiculously hung up over a guy who didn't know I existed these days, was one I preferred to ignore.

"A few of us are heading out to that new bar in town." Mia squeezed my shoulders. "Apparently there's an Aussie guy in town Kye thought you might like to meet—"

"Not interested." I held up my hand. Yeah, like that would stop these two in full matchmaking mode. "Aussie guys are footy-loving, cricket-watching, beer-swilling bogans."

"We beg to differ." Dani smirked. "The Aussie guys we know are sexy, sweet and incredibly talented in bed."

"Hear, hear," Mia said, removing her arm from my shoulders to give Dani a high-five.

"You two are pathetic." I smiled, despite a pang of loneliness making me yearn for what they'd found with Kye and Ashton. "And for your information, I'm not going."

"That's what you think," Dani said, a second before she and Mia gang-tackled me.

We tumbled to the floor amid shrieks of laughter and hair pulling.

"Get off me." I elbowed Dani hard and followed up with a well-aimed kick to Mia's shin.

"Crazy bitch," Dani said, chuckling as she sat up and

rubbed her midriff, while Mia inspected her shin. "As if a few well-aimed jabs will get you out of going tonight."

Secretly admiring their determination to avoid me turning into a hermit, I folded my arms. "You can't make me."

"Want to make a bet?" Mia smirked. "If you don't want to come for social reasons, maybe we can appeal to your professional side."

Confused, I said, "What's that supposed to mean?"

"Apparently Kye met this guy when his shoulder tendonitis flared up today." Mia's smugness made fingers of premonition strum the back of my neck. "He's a physical therapist."

No way. It couldn't be.

"What's his name?" I aimed for casual, hoping the nerves making my stomach flip-flop wouldn't affect my voice.

Mia shrugged. "No idea."

"You'll just have to come to the bar and find out," Dani said, oblivious to the rampant adrenalin flooding my system, making me want to flee.

I was being ridiculous. There were many Australian physiotherapists working around the world. The odds of this Aussie physio being Joel were a million to one.

But that didn't stop my hands from giving a betraying quiver as I snagged my long hair that had come loose in our wrestling match and twisted it into a top-knot.

"We won't take no for an answer." Mia and Dani stood next to each other, shoulders squared, determination making their eyes glitter.

"Fine, you win." I held up my hands in resignation as they did a victory jig.

"You won't regret it, sweetie," Mia said.

I already did. Because if this Aussie physio was Joel Goodes, the guy who'd broken my heart, I was in trouble. Big trouble.

JOEL

I'd had a shit of a day.

Back to back patients for eight hours straight. Four meniscectomies, three rotator cuff tears, two carpel tunnel syndromes, an Achilles tendon bursitis, ankylosing spondylitis, torticollis, Osgood-Schlatter's, synovial cyst, popliteal effusion and a hamstring tear, and that had just been the morning.

I usually thrived on the constant buzz of diagnosing and treating orthopedic injuries at the outpatient clinic I'd worked at in downtown Denver for the last three months. The manic pace suited me.

Not today. Today, I'd been too busy mulling over Mum's late night phone call to fully appreciate the varying conditions I'd treated.

Mum was considering retiring and wanted me to come home to run her practice. A good offer, if the practice had been situated anywhere but Uppity-Doo.

God, I hated that name. Hated what it stood for more. Staidness. Stability. Stifling. Small town fishbowl mentality with a healthy dose of outback narrow-mindedness. Not that Uppity-Doo was outback exactly. Situated close to the Victorian-New South Wales border, it was four hours from Melbourne. And a million miles from where I ever wanted to be.

I'd escaped the town as soon as I could. Did my physio bachelor's degree in Melbourne and had been travelling ever since. Four years on the road. Locum work from

London to LA, and many cities in between. Three months in one city was ideal, six months at a stretch.

I'd been enjoying my stint in Denver, until that phone call. Mum's bollocking, about how I'd skirted responsibility all these years, rankled. She needed someone to take over her practice. That someone couldn't be me.

So when my last patient of the day, an Aussie tennis player, had invited me to a bar with some of his mates tonight, I'd accepted. A few beers would take the edge off.

But it wouldn't eradicate the inevitable guilt that talking to Mum elicited. She sure knew how to ram the bamboo under my fingernails and hammer the buggers home. She'd been the same with Dad. And it had killed him in the end.

I entered the bar and made for the pool tables, where Kye Sheldon had said his group would be. Would be good to chat to a bunch of fellow Aussies. Not that I didn't appreciate the people I met on my travels, but nobody did laid-back humor like Aussies.

"Mate, good to see you." Kye appeared out of nowhere as I neared the tables and slapped me on the back. "Come meet the rest of the gang."

A boutique beer was thrust at me by a guy on my left. "Cheers, mate. I'm Ashton."

"Thanks." I raised the bottle in his direction. "Been in the States long?"

"About a month." Ashton pointed at Kye. "This bloke's practically a local though."

Kye grinned. "Can't tear myself away from the joint."

Ashton snorted. "That's because his girlfriend has his balls in her back pocket."

I laughed and Kye held up his hands in surrender. "Guilty as charged, and loving it."

These guys had an obvious camaraderie and I experienced a rare pang. Traveling continuously wasn't conductive to mateship and I missed having someone, anyone, I could rely on.

I'd had a good mate once, back in Uppity-Do. A mate I'd eventually lost contact with deliberately, because of what I'd done with his sister.

Man, Trevor would've killed me if he'd found out about Annabelle and me.

"You can talk." Kye pressed his thumb into Ashton's forehead. "Yep, my thumb fits perfectly into the permanent indentation Dani has left there."

Ashton clinked his beer bottle against Kye's. "I'm a schmuck in love and proud of it."

They turned to face me. "What about you, Joel? You seeing anyone?"

I shook my head. "I move around too much to maintain a relationship."

The flash of pity in their eyes surprised me. Usually guys in relationships envied my lifestyle. And freedom was enviable. Not being tied down to one woman, in one place, for all eternity. Dying a slow death.

Ashton nodded, thoughtful. "Relationships are hard work, without the added pressure of distance."

"Listen to you." Kye sniggered. "Next you'll be braiding our hair and painting our nails."

Ashton's eyes narrowed but he grinned. "Dani likes that I'm a SNAG."

"You're not a sensitive new age guy, you're a lapdog." Kye lowered his tone and leaned toward me. "He's an *artist*. That explains a lot."

In response, Ashton punched Kye on the arm. Considering the size of the tennis player's biceps I'd seen while treating his shoulder earlier today, he wouldn't feel a thing.

"Better than being a Neanderthal masquerading as a college student while playing tennis for fun." Ashton made inverted comma signs with his fingers when he said 'for fun' and smirked.

I chuckled. "You two are like an old married couple. Been mates for long?"

"A month," Kye said, which surprised me. Ashton had said he'd been in the States a month but from their obvious bond I'd assumed they'd known each other longer. "Our girlfriends are besties, so since Ashton came over with Dani for his first art show, we've been hanging around a lot."

Ashton raised his beer in Kye's direction. "But lucky for me, I'll be heading back to Melbourne in a few weeks, leaving this funny man behind."

"You'll miss me," Kye said, deadpan.

"Like a hole in the head," Ashton muttered, his amused gaze drawn to the door behind me. "Don't look now, Sheldon, but your balls just made an appearance."

Kye elbowed Ashton and the artist winced a little.

"About time the girls showed up," Kye said, waving. "Don't worry, mate, they've brought a friend so you won't feel like a third wheel."

Shit, this better not be some lame fix-up. I wanted to have a few beers to unwind, not feel compelled to make mindless small talk with some chick I wouldn't see after tonight.

"She's a real hottie, too," Ashton said, elbowing me. "Check her out."

I glanced over my shoulder, the epitome of casual, and froze.

Because I knew the petite redhead with the killer bod striding toward me. Knew her intimately. And damned if my cock didn't harden at the memory.

Annabelle Cleary. The only good thing to come out of Uppity-Doo. And one of the reasons I'd bolted as fast as I goddamned could from that shithole town.

Kye bumped me. "What do you think?"

I am so screwed.

READ THE REST NOW!

ABOUT THE AUTHOR

USA TODAY bestselling and multi-award winning author Nicola Marsh writes page-turning fiction to keep you up all night.

She's published 82 books and writes contemporary romance, domestic suspense, and fantasy.

She's also a Waldenbooks, Bookscan, Amazon, iBooks, and Barnes & Noble bestseller, a RBY (Romantic Book of the Year) and National Readers' Choice Award winner, and a multi-finalist for numerous other awards, including the RITA.

A physiotherapist for thirteen years, she now adores writing full time, raising her two dashing young heroes, barracking loudly for her Kangaroos football team, sharing fine food with family and friends, and her favorite, curling up with a good book!

Printed in Great Britain
by Amazon